AMBIGUITY AND LOGIC

In this book, Frederic Schick extends and applies the decision theory he proposed in two previous Cambridge books: *Understanding Action* (1991) and *Making Choices* (1997). He shows how the way we see situations affects the choices we make, and he develops a logic of thought responsive to how things are seen.

The book considers many questions of choosing and some familiar human predicaments. Why do people in choice experiments act so often against expectations? How might they and the experimenters be looking at different problems in them? Why do people cooperate so often where the textbook logic excludes that? How can there be weakness of will – and must it always be faulted? Does how we see things affect what they *mean,* and what are people reporting who say that their lives have no meaning for them? These very different questions turn out to have some closely related answers.

There are vivid discussions here of cases drawn from many sources. The book will interest all who study how we choose and act, whether they are philosophers, psychologists, or economists – or any combination.

Frederic Schick is Professor of Philosophy at Rutgers University.

Ambiguity and Logic

FREDERIC SCHICK

PUBLISHED BY THE PRESS SYNDICATE OF THE UNIVERSITY OF CAMBRIDGE
The Pitt Building, Trumpington Street, Cambridge, United Kingdom

CAMBRIDGE UNIVERSITY PRESS
The Edinburgh Building, Cambridge CB2 2RU, UK
40 West 20th Street, New York, NY 10011-4211, USA
477 Williamstown Road, Port Melbourne, VIC 3207, Australia
Ruiz de Alarcón 13, 28014 Madrid, Spain
Dock House, The Waterfront, Cape Town 8001, South Africa

http://www.cambridge.org

First published 2003

Printed in the United States of America

Typeface Meridien 10/13 pt. *System* LaTeX 2ε [TB]

A catalog record for this book is available from the British Library.

Library of Congress Cataloging in Publication Data

Schick, Frederic, 1929–
Ambiguity and logic / Frederic Schick.
p. cm.
Includes bibliographical references (p.) and index.
ISBN 0 521 82458 3 – ISBN 0 521 53171 3 (pb.)
1. Decision making. 2. Ambiguity. 3. Logic. I. Title.
BD184 .S335 2003
128′. 4–dc21 2002035199

ISBN 0 521 82458 3 hardback
ISBN 0 521 53171 3 paperback

for Kay, yet again

CONTENTS

PREFACE

EACH of the essays in this book was written during the past five years. Only two have been published elsewhere. Each can be read on its own. Still, they were meant to be read in sequence; Essay 1 is general, Essay 2 more narrowly focused, Essay 3 more technical, etc. In a wholly perfect world, they would be read in the order presented.

An earlier version of Essay 3 appeared in *Economics and Philosophy* of 1999 (as "Status Quo Basing and the Logic of Value"). An earlier version of Essay 5 appeared in *The Journal of Philosophy* of 2000 (as "Surprise, Self-Knowledge, and Commonality"). Essay 2 is a revised version of a paper that will appear in *Synthese*. I thank the editors and publishers of these journals for their permission to reprint these papers.

Each of these papers, or some earlier version, has been presented to one or another academic group, at Lund University and Uppsala University in Sweden, at Cambridge University in England, at Columbia, the Graduate Center of the City University of New York, the University of Arizona, the New School University, and others in the United States. I thank the audiences at these meetings for their lively and useful discussions.

Finally, a special thanks to my friends – they know who they are – who have encouraged me in this. And a very special thanks to those who encouraged me though they weren't persuaded.

1

LIVING WITH AMBIGUITY

SAY we are fully informed. Say we know all we could possibly know. Still, there remains ambiguity. What we now do is ambiguous, and what that will bring about is too, and so is all that would have happened if we had done something else instead. How we act in any setting depends on how we there get around this, on how we disambiguate there. And our later making sense of our actions calls for our knowing how we did it.

1

Let me begin with some stories that may help to bring that out. The first will be about me, and it will do me little credit.

When this happened, I was thirty and on my first good job. I then had two particular friends – call them Adam and Bob. Adam was lively and good-looking. Women liked him and he liked women. Bob too liked women, but they cared for him less, and he ached for what Adam had. He would always ask about Adam, hoping at least to feed fantasies, but I knew nothing he wanted to hear, so I couldn't oblige him.

Then, one day, I did. To his "What's new with Adam?" I said "He moved; he had to." Bob asked why. "Because it was three o'clock in the morning and he had the music on loud, and the landlord came up from downstairs" – I was making all this up – "...and found him in bed with two women and evicted him."

Bob was staggered and went home in a sweat. I thought it funny and went to tell Adam, but it turned out he wasn't in town, and he still was out of town when I saw Bob the next time. Right off, Bob asked about Adam, and I made up a new story for him about how Adam had thrown a big party to celebrate his new apartment and how the noise got the police to be called and how they responded to what the guests, both dressed and undressed, were doing. Bob could hardly breathe for excitement.

A few days later, Adam called. He began with "Are you out of your mind?", and with that the scales fell from my eyes. I had no answer to give him. I was now the one who was staggered; what I had done did now seem crazy and I could scarcely credit having done it. All of us taught at a straight-laced college, and Adam was up for promotion just then. The stories I was telling about him were enough to get him fired instead. I had known that all along. I knew I was putting his job at risk but I did it anyway, and thought it funny as I did it. I saw it as a joke, as pulling Bob's leg, as horsing around with friends.

I had seen what I did as a joke; now I saw it as a kind of betrayal. But that made no change in what I *believed* I had done, in what I *knew* about that. Neither did it change what I wanted. I wanted before to joke with my friends, and I still wanted that. I wanted now not to injure them, but I had wanted that before too. What changed was how I *saw* things – again, Adam's call refocused my mind: it gave me a new perspective. Had I seen things that way before, I would not have done what I did. Still, how could a change of perspective alone have unsettled what moved me to act? The usual theory of motivation – the usual theory of reasons for action – speaks of beliefs and desires only. How did the way I came to see things connect with the beliefs and desires I had?

Enough about Adam and Bob. Let me turn to an incident I have discussed at length before,[1] this one reported by George Orwell in an essay on the Spanish Civil War. Orwell tells of lying in wait in a field one day, hoping for a chance to shoot at some soldiers in the trenches ahead. For a long time, no one appeared. Then some planes flew over, which took the Fascists by surprise, there was much shouting and blowing of whistles, and a man

> ...jumped out of the trench and ran along the top of the parapet in full view. He was half-dressed and was holding up his trousers with both hands as he ran. I refrained from shooting at him.... I did not shoot partly because of that detail about the trousers. I had come here to shoot at "Fascists"; but a man holding up his trousers isn't a "Fascist," he is visibly a fellow-creature, similar to yourself, and you don't feel like shooting at him.[2]

Orwell wanted to "shoot at Fascists" and he believed he now could do it. On the belief/desire theory, he had a solid reason for shooting. What then was it about those pants that got him to put down his gun? Orwell answers that question: "a man holding up his trousers ... is visibly a fellow-creature, similar to yourself." I take it the pants were down to his knees, and that Orwell is saying that someone half-naked and "visibly" human had to be seen as human. Before the man jumped out of the trench, Orwell had seen his firing at him as shooting at a fascist, which he wanted to do. The soldier's half-naked predicament was for him a wake-up call – like Adam's call to me. He then saw his firing at him as his shooting at a fellow-creature, and this he didn't "feel like" doing.

He had, of course, known all along that, under their pants, the fascists were human. He had never *faced* that fact, never fully confronted it, but how did his not having faced it weaken the force of his knowing it? And how could he want to kill a fascist and also not *feel like* doing it? How can a change in a person's seeings undercut what he wants to do?

The third story here is fictional, though it recalls an actual case and is formally like many others.[3] Jack and Jill are at a company banquet. Recent employees and the youngest ones there, they are seated in a corner of the room, where they notice, while the others are eating, that they hadn't been served.

The kitchen had run out of food. They were least likely to make a fuss and so had been picked for doing without.

Jill suggests that they leave and get burgers. Jack is firmly opposed. He says he has paid $50 for dinner and won't pay a nickel more. Jill says the $50 is spent and gone; the question is whether to leave and get a $5 burger or starve. Jack insists she has that wrong: the question is whether to pay $55 and get just a burger or starve. Fifty-five dollars is too much for dinner, never mind for a burger dinner – he prefers to starve. They argue this back and forth. In the end, they go out to eat.

How did Jill move Jack? (It was too early for hunger to have done it.) He had a belief/desire reason both for staying and for leaving. He wanted not to pay $55 for dinner and he knew he wouldn't pay that if he stayed. But he also wanted a burger and knew that leaving meant getting one. Jill didn't change his beliefs; she told him nothing he didn't know. Nor did she get him to agree with her judgment of what a burger was worth. He agreed with her all along that a burger was worth $5. What she did was to get him to stop seeing that burger as a $55 dinner – she got him to see it as a *$5* dinner. She changed his perspective on leaving to get it. But how did his new view of leaving unsettle the reason he had for staying?

2

I have presented three cases – my leg-pulling prank, Orwell's putting down his gun, Jack's leaving to get a burger. In none does the belief/desire theory fully explain what happened. On that two-factor theory, a person has a reason for taking action *a* where he wants to take an action of a certain sort *b* and he believes *a* is of sort *b*. I wanted to play a joke on Bob and believed I was doing that. But I also wanted to be a proper friend of Adam's and knew that this called for some self-restraint. I had as good a two-factor reason for holding back as for doing what I did. Why then did I not hold back? Likewise for Orwell and for Jack. They too had belief/desire reasons both for doing what they did and for doing the opposite. Why then did they act in one way and not in the other instead?

The belief/desire theory of reasons must be refined in some way, and I think we can't just refine it by speaking of *intensities* of desire. We can't just say that Orwell wanted to avoid his killing "fellow creatures" more than he wanted to kill Fascists, that Jack wanted a burger more than he wanted not to pay $55 for dinner, etc. That would only give us more questions. Why should a man's holding up his pants have changed the relative strengths of Orwell's desires? Why should that phone call from Adam have changed the relative strengths of mine? Did our desires (their strengths) change at all? No doubt they *may* have changed, but why should one think that they did?

I will take a different line. In my report of each of these cases, I described the people in them as getting a new perspective on things. I spoke of how some event or discussion changed the way they *saw* things. What was it there that changed? I had seen my teasing Bob as a joke, but that wasn't like my seeing that his face became flushed. Orwell's seeing the fascist before him as a fellow human being – his seeing that to shoot would be to shoot a human being – wasn't like seeing he was running. The *seeing* in these cases was conceptual. We might describe it as a *conceiving* of the action (of the joshing or the shooting), and this conceptual seeing or understanding calls for being fitted-in somehow. I propose replacing the two-factor, belief/desire theory of reasons with this three-factor refinement of it, that a person has a reason for taking action *a* where he wants to take an action of a certain sort *b* (one that *leads to* or *brings about* or simply *is* a *b*) and he believes *a* is of sort *b* – *and* he sees or understands *a* as being of that sort (as leading to or bringing about . . . *b*). A reason for taking action *a* is a belief-and-desire-plus-seeing.

More should be said about *seeings* or *understandings*.[4] Let me just say here that we can, at any moment, see *a* in one way only, though that way may be compound; *a* might be seen as of sort *b*-and-*b*′-and-*b*″. And that our seeing *a* in some way implies that we have the corresponding belief. If we see *a* as of sort *b*, we must *believe* it is of that sort, though not all we believe about it has to enter our view of it. Isn't this still then a two-factor theory, the factors being *seeing* and *desire*, the belief here implicit in the seeing? I will continue to speak of three factors because our beliefs, desires, and seeings are distinct mental states that we have and they all figure in our reasons. But, again, our beliefs and our seeings aren't logically independent. (If we see *a* as a *b*, we must *believe* it is a *b*, perhaps a *b*-and-*b*′.)

Our beliefs and desires alone don't give us a reason for action. Only a belief and a desire plus a related seeing do that. Before the soldier appeared, Orwell had a reason to shoot. He thought that shooting would kill a fascist, he wanted to kill a fascist, and he saw his shooting as his killing a fascist. But facing the man holding up his pants, he no longer saw it so, and his reason came apart; he still wanted to kill a fascist, but he didn't "feel like" killing this one. Jack had seen paying $5 for a burger as the last payment on a huge bill for his dinner; when he ceased to see it that way, he lost his reason for not leaving. In the case of my joke with Bob, I came to stop seeing it as a joke. I then no longer had the reason that had led me to make it.

Putting all this differently, every action might be seen in any number of ways: in that sense, each is *ambiguous*.[5] Orwell might have seen the shooting as his shooting a fascist or as shooting a "fellow creature." He did in fact see it the latter way, and seeing it that way disambiguated it for him. He disambiguated *not* then shooting as *not* hurting a fellow man. Given what he believed and wanted (he wanted to avoid hurting fellow creatures), he had a reason to put down his gun. A person has a reason for action *a* where he believes *a* is of sort *b*, he wants to take an action of that sort, and he sees, he *disambiguates a* as *b*.

It has been said that any action can have different *meanings* for people, for different people at the same time and the same person at different times. Different perspectives yield different meanings. To see an action in this way or that – to disambiguate what we might do – is to assign a certain *meaning* to it.[6] Thus whether or not we take action *a* depends on what it *means* to us, and the point might be put like this: one of the factors of our reason for *a* is the meaning *a* has for us. I will avoid the language of *meanings*, but it may give some readers a handle on my concept of reasons.

3

What I have said about reasons for actions carries over to reasons for choices. Our choices often have reasons too, and how we see those choices figures in our reasons for making them. Why did we *choose* to take action *a*? Perhaps we chose it because we believed that it was a *rational* action, we wanted to take a rational action, and we saw it as being rational. But our seeings sometimes also enter in a second way here, for they bear on the question of which of the actions we might take would be rational.

Suppose you have some benefit you must give either to Jack or to Jill. It must go to one or the other. It can't be divided between them. Say that the benefit is a job, that you don't care which of them gets it, and that you have three options: you might give it right off to Jack, you might give it right off to Jill, or you might toss a coin. Many people would reach for the coin. That is the fair way to do it, and most people, in such cases, prefer (and take steps) to be fair.

This scenario has troubled choice theorists for a number of years. The problem they find is this. You set the same utility on Jack's getting the job as on its going to Jill; let that utility be x. If you toss the coin, the job is as likely to go to one as to the other. The expected utility of tossing that coin is therefore $\frac{1}{2}x + \frac{1}{2}x$, and this too is x. So you should be indifferent between tossing the coin and either outright hire. If you *aren't* indifferent – if you insist on tossing that coin – you have turned against rationality. Does this mean that being rational calls for indifference between fairness and unfairness?[7]

Here is a very different question that is formally similar. (The difference is only that there are two options in this and not three.) The question comes up near the end of Tolstoy's *War and Peace*. Two commanders of guerillas are discussing what they do with the prisoners they take. Denisov sends his prisoners to the regular army camp, many days' march away. Dolohov does not send his off. He says,

> "You send off a hundred prisoners and hardly more than a couple of dozen arrive. The rest either die of starvation or get killed. So isn't it just as well to make short work of them? . . ."
>
> "That's not the point [says Denisov]. . . . I don't care to have their lives on my conscience. You say they die on the road. All right. Only it's not my doing."[8]

Let the prospects be even more grim: *all* the prisoners die on the road. Looking just at these people's lives, the outcomes are then exactly the same whether the prisoners are sent off or shot. When we add the risk to the troops sent to guard the prisoners and we go by the outcomes, we have no choice but to shoot them. That would be Dolohov's view of it. Denisov wouldn't shoot even here, which squares with Dolohov's thinking him a squeamish, soft-headed fool.

Must we agree with Dolohov's judgment? Rational choosers go by the outcomes: they are consequentialists. Yes, but that doesn't settle it, for we must look at *how* they go by them, how their thinking connects with those outcomes, how certain values they set on the outcomes get wired-up in their thinking.

On what do our desires, preferences, and utilities – collectively, our values – focus? What are the *objects* of those values? Say that I want to be king of France. There is then something here I want (something my wanting takes as its *object*). But that something can't be the situation of my now being the king, for there is no such situation. What I want is that *I become king,* and this describes or *reports* a situation, actual or just possible. A report of a situation sometimes is called a *proposition,* and we can say that the values we have take propositions as objects.

Propositions may be thought of as (in part) like abstractions, like numbers or relations: they have no spatial or temporal locus but can, where true, be locally instanced. They are then instanced by what they report, which makes them also unlike abstractions: there are many instances of the relation *larger than,* but a (simple, noncompound) proposition can't report more than one situation. If p and q report different situations, p and q are different propositions.[9] Where we both want that *Jack gets the job* but we are thinking of different Jacks, what we want is different too. Still (again), we cannot say that what we want are the situations themselves, or that what we want is built up somehow of situations (or of certain Jacks plus . . .). We can distinguish what we want from what we don't by what is "out there" somewhere, but we can't go on to infer that what we want is "not in our heads" – unless we mean only that propositions, as abstract objects, are nowhere at all.[10]

About the outcome of an action, this holds that the outcome isn't valued in its brute natural state. It is valued *as it appears in these or those propositions.* Putting the point another way: we value an outcome always *under these or those reports of it.* Or, in terms of *descriptions*: what we believe about an outcome allows for many descriptions of it, and we sometimes set different values on the same outcomes *under different descriptions.* Which of these values then enter our thinking – which of them get wired up? I think the answer has to be this, that the values that count for us are those that we set on the outcomes described as we see those outcomes.[11]

A rational chooser goes by the outcomes, by certain values he sets on them. But these values are the ones he sets on the outcomes *as he sees them;* other people, equally rational, who see them differently, may make different choices. Dolohov saw all the possible outcomes in terms of how many prisoners would wind up dead; that argued for their being shot. Denisov too saw the outcome of sending them off to the camp as their dying on the road. But he saw the outcome of shooting them not as their dying but as his having killed them. He resisted the latter outcome, *as he saw that outcome*; he didn't want it "on his conscience." He preferred the other, *as he saw that*. Both Dolohov and Denisov chose rationally. They both went by the outcomes, by how they saw the outcomes. The difference in what they did had to do with *how* they saw the outcomes.

So too in our hiring story. Are you being soft-headed if you choose to toss that coin, if you *prefer* to toss it? In this case also, that depends. If you see the outcomes solely in terms of which person gets the job, tossing the coin is pointless for you. For since you don't care which of them gets it, you value all the outcomes of tossing and not-tossing, as you see them, the same. But if you see the possible outcomes of tossing the coin in a fuller way – as Jack's or Jill's getting that job because of how fairness worked out in their case – and if you value fairness, you prefer the so-seen outcomes of tossing the coin to those of not tossing (as you see *those*). If you are rational, you will toss that coin; you then *have* to toss it. No soft-headedness there.

4

What about someone thinking of how certain other people are choosing? If he ignores how the others see things, he will often misjudge them. He will take his own perspective to be shared by these other people and will judge the rationality of their choices by whether he would have made them. That will then often lead him to think these others themselves not rational.

Here is what is called Zeckhauser's problem.[12] You are being held captive by a lunatic who threatens to force you to shoot yourself with a fully loaded six-shooter unless you pay him a ransom – if you pay, he will empty one chamber before

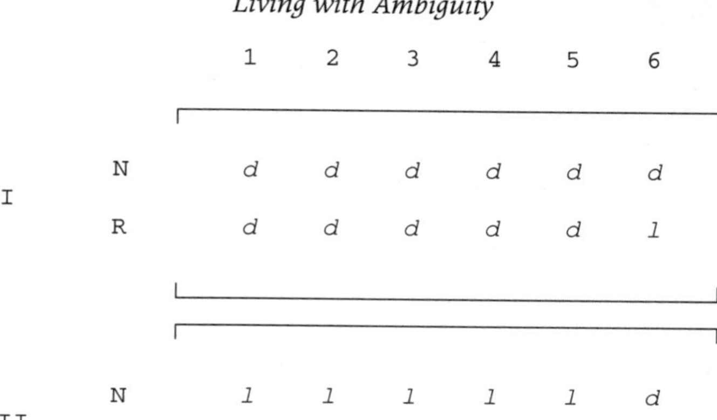

Figure 1.1

you must spin the cylinder and shoot. That is his threat in the mornings. In the evenings, he relents; he empties five of the chambers and offers also to empty the sixth if you pay a ransom. There are two cases to think about here. You are willing to pay in both. Would you pay more in one than in the other? If so, in which case would you pay more?

If you think as most people do, you would pay more in the second than the first.[13] Paying more in the second case seems to make good sense, for in the first case your paying a ransom would only lower your risk of dying while in the second it would keep you alive. Still, on a common analysis, rationality argues against this. Whatever you are willing to pay in one case, you should be willing to pay in the other. For the expected-utility value of your paying-a-ransom option (of the proposition *I pay a ransom*) exceeds that of your not-ransoming option by the same in both cases.

Look at Figure 1.1. I and II are the two cases. The columns stand for the chambers that might be either loaded or not. If you fire a loaded chamber, the outcome is death (*d* is *I die*); if

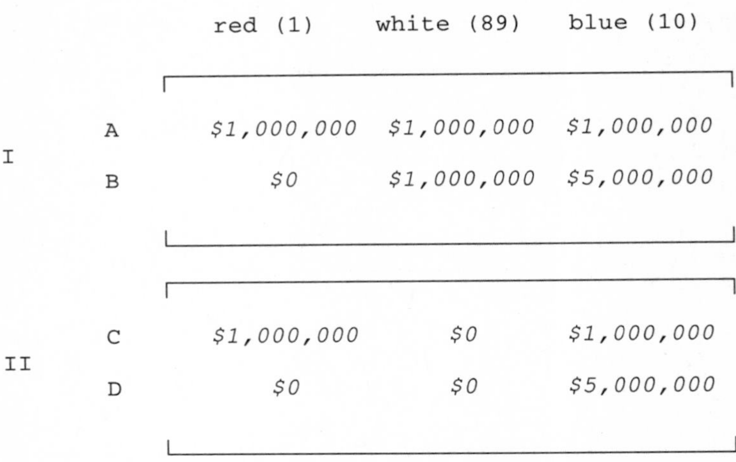

		red (1)	white (89)	blue (10)
I	A	$1,000,000	$1,000,000	$1,000,000
	B	$0	$1,000,000	$5,000,000
II	C	$1,000,000	$0	$1,000,000
	D	$0	$0	$5,000,000

Figure 1.2

you fire an empty one, the outcome is life (*l* is *I live*). R is the option of ransoming, N is that of not-ransoming. In case I, the expected-utility value of N is $u(d)$; that of R is $5/6u(d) + 1/6u(l)$. Subtracting the latter from the former yields $1/6u(d) - 1/6u(l)$. In case II, the expected utility of N is $5/6u(l) + 1/6u(d)$; that of R is $u(l)$. The difference again is $1/6u(d) - 1/6u(l)$. So you should be willing to pay the same in both cases for the better option R. Since most people would pay more in the second, most people wouldn't be rational.

Before I put in a word for these people, let me describe a related problem, the so-called Allais' paradox.[14] This appears in Figure 1.2. Again there are two cases, in each of which you have two options. In case I, if you take option A, you will get a million dollars. If you take B, what you will get depends on the color of a ball that will be drawn from an urn. If that ball is red, you will get nothing; if it is white, you will get a million dollars; if it is blue, you will get five million. In case II, if you take option C, you will get a million dollars if the ball drawn is either red or blue; if it is white, you will get nothing. If you take D, you will get five million dollars if the ball is blue; if it is not, you will get nothing. You know that there are 100 balls, one of them red, 89 white, and 10 blue.

Which options would you choose in these cases? It seems that most people choose A in case I and choose D in case II. But notice that, in both these cases, if a white ball is drawn, the outcomes of both options are the same. So, in both cases, which of the options has the greater expected utility depends just on the outcomes if that ball is either red or blue; and in these two situations, cases I and II are identical. This means that the expected utility of A can't be greater than that of B unless that of C is greater than that of D. Again: most people choose A and D. So if we think of rationality as the maximizing of expected utility, here too most people aren't rational.[15]

Is this judgment correct? It assumes that the people involved believe that the outcomes are those announced and that they value money (the more, the better), and this needn't be doubted. But it also assumes that they see the outcomes as these are described to them, in money terms only. That is the way those making the judgment see the outcomes here, but perhaps the A-and-D choosers see these outcomes differently.

How do the choosers of A and D account for their choosing as they do? They say that, in case II, both options are risky and that, all in all, they prefer D, but that, in I, though B is risky, A is a sure million dollars. If they chose B and the ball is red, they would be going home empty-handed when they could, whatever the color, have had a cool million if they chose A – they say that, in I, that settles it for them. This suggests that, looking at B, they don't see its zero-outcome in money terms only but also (in part) counterfactually, as that zero-money payoff minus the opportunity cost. They see it not as *I get nothing* but as *I get nothing when I was sure to get a million if I had chosen A*, and they set a lower utility on the latter proposition than on the former.

Their issues should then be reported as in Figure 1.3, which is like Figure 1.2 except for the *$0/w*-entry, *$0/w* being short for

		red (1)	white (89)	blue (10)
I	A	*$1,000,000*	*$1,000,000*	*$1,000,000*
	B	*$0/w*	*$1,000,000*	*$5,000,000*
II	C	*$1,000,000*	*$0*	*$1,000,000*
	D	*$0*	*$0*	*$5,000,000*

Figure 1.3

I get nothing when I was sure to get a million if I had chosen A. If they set a sufficiently low utility on *$0/w*, A has a greater expected utility for them than does B. If, in addition, the expected utility of D exceeds that of C, their choosing both A and D is rational. People who fault these choices, who hold that they *can't* be rational, see the outcomes as in Figure 1.2 and assume that the choosers do too: they are imposing their own way of seeing on the people they are faulting.

Likewise in Zeckhauser's problem. Many people will pay much more to get the only loaded chamber emptied than to get their captor to empty just one of the loaded six. Can these people be rational? Yes, for they may see the dying-outcome in case II not as *I die* but as *I die when I was sure to live if I had paid the ransom*. If so, their issues should be reported as in Figure 1.4, in which *d/w* is *I die when I was sure to live....*[16] Suppose, as is likely, they set a lower utility on *d/w* than on *d* simpliciter. The expected utility of R then exceeds that of N in case II by more than it does in case I, which calls for paying more in II than in I. The critics who fault the thinking of those who would indeed pay more are seeing the outcomes as in Figure 1.1 and failing

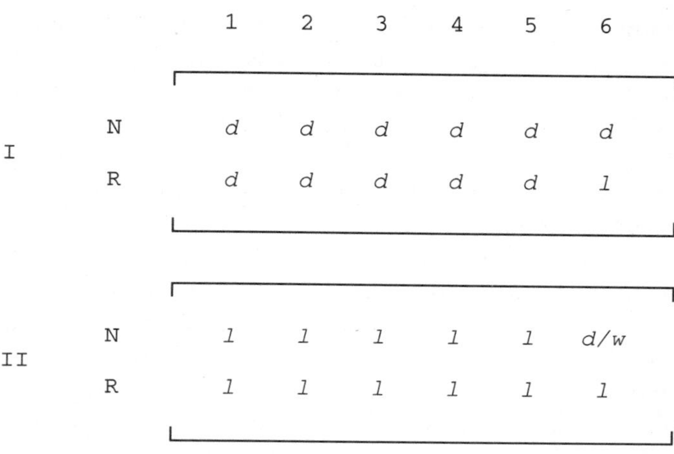

Figure 1.4

to allow for their being seen as these people may in fact see them.

I have argued that the concept of reasons must find a role for how things are seen, that we must move from a two-factor theory to a three-factor theory of reasons. The cases here (and in the section just above) suggest a like refinement of the theory of rationality. A person choosing rationally chooses an option that maximizes his expected utility, the probability-weighted average of the utilities of its possible outcomes. But outcomes can be differently described (think of the *d* and *d/w* descriptions), and we set utilities on them only as described in this way or that. And we sometimes set different utilities on the same outcome differently described (again, think of *d* and *d/w*). Which of these utilities then enter our thinking? Those that focus on the outcome described *as we see that outcome*. So, yes, a person choosing rationally chooses an option that maximizes his expected utility, but that is now the probability-weighted average of the utilities of the outcomes *as he sees them.*[17]

Some writers don't agree that a given outcome might be differently described. They hold instead that different descriptions mark out different outcomes. John Broome speaks of *individuation*: every description (and thus every seeing) individuates a different outcome. That idea comes to this, that outcomes are different if and only if the propositions that describe them are different.[18]

For Broome, *d* and *d/w* are different outcomes, not the same outcome under different descriptions. Still, in some sense, they must be the same, the same under different descriptions. If just one of the chambers is loaded and you now fire that chamber, they would report the same *event*, the same *causal effect* of your firing; both *d* and *d/w* would report your death, and you only could have died once. (The "*/w*" clause doesn't bring in any added effect of your firing.) I hold that events are independent of how it is we describe them, that what marks them off from each other are their causal connections.[19] But no need to insist on causal individuation here. The point is that a rational person attends to the outcomes as he sees them, however they are marked out.

Pulling it all together now in terms of ambiguity, here are four points I have made. Our actions are always ambiguous, and so (*pace* Broome) are the possible outcomes of any action we might take. Whether we have a *reason* for *a* depends on how we disambiguate *a*, on how we *see* that action. Whether our choosing it would be *rational* depends on how we disambiguate its outcomes (and the outcomes of our other options). And theories of reasons and of rationality that ignore ambiguity often misjudge people.

5

Most theories today ignore it.[20] Still, some writers study some issues along the lines I have sketched. They show how, in this or that case, certain so-called deviant choices might be explained, and held to be rational, if we took note of how the choosers interpret (how they *see*) the outcomes in that case.[21] There is also a common objection to this occasional way of thinking – to the approach that I am saying ought to be generalized.

The objection is that such thinking leaves the theory of rationality vacuous. Here is Amos Tversky on the subject: "In the absence of any constraints [on how the outcomes may be described], the consequences [outcomes] can always be interpreted so as to satisfy the axioms."[22] Here is Mark Machina: "... [I]nvoking a right [to reinterpret the outcomes] is tantamount to defending the expected utility model by rendering it irrefutable."[23] Whatever action a person chooses, he can always describe the outcomes so as to make his choice rational.

Allowing for different "interpretations" lets us endorse different choices. But the same holds for utilities and probabilities: different utility and probability settings also let us endorse different choices. Would it be rational for a Zeckhauser captive to refuse to pay any ransom whatever? Yes, if he sets the same utility on living as on dying. Would he be rational if he refused to pay a nickel in the first case (where paying would leave five chambers loaded) but would pay a million in the second (where then none would be loaded)? Yes, if he took the probability to be 1 that, if any chambers stayed loaded, he would trigger one of those. Could a person rationally choose B and C in Allais' problem? Yes, if he didn't care about money.

This doesn't render the theory vacuous; it doesn't say that whatever one chooses can be held to be rational. It says only that any choice would be rational for a chooser in some frame of mind. *Your* frame of mind very likely is different from those imagined above. You set more utility on living than on dying, your probabilities aren't paranoid, and you care about money. A rational person in *your* frame of mind must pay some ransom even in the first Zeckhauser case (either six or five chambers loaded). So if *you* won't pay anything, you are not being rational.

Likewise with how you describe the outcomes. No description is rationalizing for you unless it puts things *as you see them*. If you see the dying-outcome of case II as *I die*, rationality calls for your paying the same ransom in case II as in I (assuming nonmorbid utilities and nonparanoid probabilities). You could also describe that outcome as *I die when I was sure to live . . .* , but that wouldn't make it rational to pay a bigger ransom in II unless you came to *see* it that way. And you can't change how you see things at will, no more so than you can change your beliefs and desires (or your utilities and probabilities) at will. A theory that attends to a person's seeings gives different directives to people in different mind-sets. But it issues *specific* directives to people in this or that mind-set, and so it isn't vacuous.

Let me briefly comment too on a second critique, this one directed at my own theory but applying to every project of allowing for selective seeings. In a review of my *Making Choices*, Brian Skyrms says that it may be good psychology but that it isn't choice theory, ". . . twentieth-century rational choice theory [having] been developed not as psychology but as *logic* – the logic of consistent choice behaviour."[24] He refers to my example of Macbeth, who resisted killing the king when he saw it as treachery, as the murder of his kinsman and guest, but lunged ahead when he saw it as boldness. Skyrms takes such selective seeings (the killing *as this*, the killing *as that*) to be clear lapses of rationality. A rational Macbeth would have seen what he did under "all its aspects known to him – at least [as] 'boldly seizing power by murdering my kinsman, my king and my guest.' This is a requirement enforced by orthodox rational decision theory."[25] People often are like Macbeth (and like Orwell and the others); so, as psychology, my theory is sound. But, where they are, they are confused, for it isn't sound logic.

Tversky spoke of the need for constraints on how situations are described. Skyrms suggests that logic imposes this constraint of *total belief*, that all we believe about a situation has to be part of how we now see it. Only our *logical* seeings matter where we are being rational, and a logical view of things takes in all we believe about them. This means that our seeings can't focus our minds (or can't more narrowly than our beliefs already do), that they can't be selective. Proper logic denies them that role.

Must we accept the total-belief constraint? Many people would say *no*, and some would resist it on principled grounds. Consider adherents of *welfarism*, of the idea that what counts in an outcome is how well people fare in it, that we should look to people's well-being and to nothing else. People who hold to this idea reject the total-belief constraint, for that would commit them to taking account of much they consider not relevant, much that is other than welfare. Think also of those who hold that only the *actuality* of outcomes may count, that how we see an outcome may not take in what *might* just have happened (as in Figures 1.3 and 1.4). These people too reject the total-belief constraint.

This in itself settles nothing. Welfarism and actualism and other such ideas are controversial; many people reject *them*. Denisov rejected welfarism (he wouldn't have shot his prisoners even if that would have saved some lives), and many people involved in an Allais or Zeckhauser problem reject actualism. Still, are these people speaking for logic? Are all selective seeings illogical? One could hold that they are; that the total-belief constraint is indeed a principle of logic, that it is logical bedrock. But this would only beg the question of the status of selective seeings. It would prejudge that question; it couldn't be taken to settle it. It could not discredit a logic that allows for selective seeings – for Macbeth's and Orwell's seeings and our various others'. Let us here leave the question open. It calls for a fuller discussion.[26]

That I take a stand against logic might be argued from another direction. We set utilities on propositions without regard to how we now see things. Our seeings come in independently: they select the propositions the utilities of which then count for us. Our seeings may even select propositions whose utilities differ from those that we set on others we think report the same. In such a case, the way we see things selects from the different values we set on what we think are the same situations (differently described). It makes some values we have operative for us and not other values we have.

On my theory, this not only happens but it needn't be faulted. Some will say that it goes against logic. It goes against this principle of *extensionality,* that if you think that *x* and *y* report the same situation, you cannot value them differently. This is not a constraint on seeings (like Skyrmsian totalism), but on valuations. Must we accept the constraint? No good case is ever made for it, so I feel free to reject it.[27]

A deeper issue is that of what logic we are speaking of here. What (sort of a) logic constrains people's values? What (sort of a) logic constrains people's *seeings*? Logics of value (of utilities, etc.) have been around a long time. Logics of belief are familiar too. What are the principles of a logic of seeings – a logic of ambiguity? And how does it relate to the others? These too are questions we must shelve for a while.[28]

2

A DILEMMA FOR WHOM?

JACK and Jill have been arrested. The District Attorney now tells them this. They can either talk or keep silent. If they both talk, they will each get a ten-year sentence. If one of them talks (confessing for both) and the other does not, the one who talked will go free; the other will get a twenty-year sentence. If they both keep silent, each will get a one-year sentence on some trumped-up charge. The DA makes sure they believe him. Then he puts them in separate cells and goes to take their pleas.

1

Say that neither Jack nor Jill has any idea of what the other will do but that each supposes that it doesn't depend on what *he* (she) will do. Also that neither expects to meet the other again at some future time, or to meet the other's cousins in a dark alley somewhere. Also that neither cares at all about how the other makes out; each cares only about the length of his (her) own stay in jail. This lets each map his (her) own problem as in Figure 2.1.

Jack is here the row-chooser, Jill the column-chooser – *S* is staying silent, *T* is talking. Each number-pair refers to the outcome of one of the possible action-pairs, the first number being Jack's ranking of that outcome, the second being Jill's (the larger the number, the higher the ranking). The rankings reveal that talking is the dominant option for both: each would do better by talking, whatever the other did. So if Jack and Jill are both rational, both of them will talk. But since each prefers

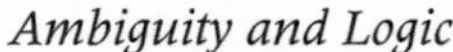

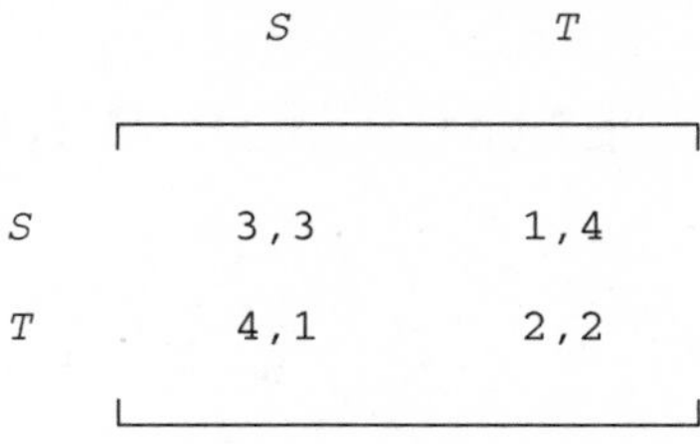

	S	T
S	3,3	1,4
T	4,1	2,2

Figure 2.1

the outcome of *S,S* (both of them silent) to that of *T,T*, they will both be sorry.

This is the familiar Prisoners' Dilemma, the basis of countless recent discussions of the logic of interaction. In a case of the sort above that they map as in Figure 2.1, both Jack and Jill, if they act rationally, will wish that they both hadn't: the outcome will be Pareto-suboptimal. This cannot be got around. Still, a premise here is that they map their situation as in Figure 2.1, and they need not map it so.

Look at it first from Jack's point of view. Jill might act either one way or the other. This means there are two contingencies. Figure 2.1 identifies these as *Jill keeps silent* (*S*) and *She talks* (*T*), but suppose that Jack in fact partitions the contingency field differently. As he puts it to himself, either *A* or *O* holds: either *Jill will do as I will* (*A*) or *She will do the opposite* (*O*). (Better, *A* is *Whichever of silence/talking describes what I will do, the same describes what Jill will,* and *O* is *Whichever of that pair describes what I will do, the other describes what Jill will.*) *A* is that Jill will act as Jack will, that she will do that *unwittingly*; it isn't that she will tit-for-tat – that she will follow Jack's lead. (She won't find out what he did till later!) Correspondingly for *O*.

Jack, again, has no idea of what Jill will be doing, of which of the two, *A* and *O*, is true (he sets no probabilities on them). But he supposes them independent probabilistically of what *he* will do. He supposes the contingencies he faces, here *A* and *O*, independent of his own actions. Recalling now what the DA

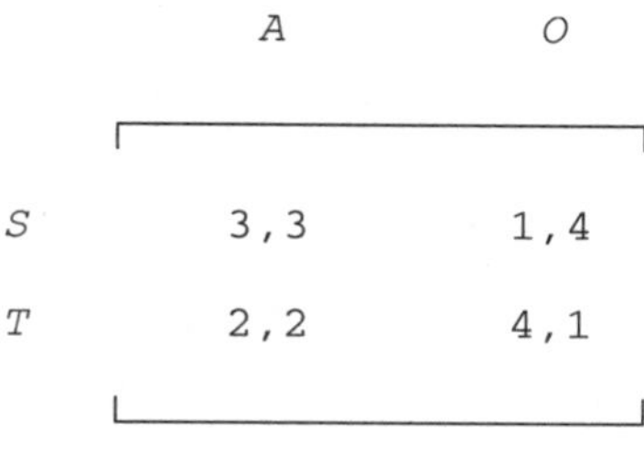

	A	O
S	3,3	1,4
T	2,2	4,1

Figure 2.2

said gives us Figure 2.2. Jack has no dominant option here: he now *needn't* talk (confess). He remains free to talk, but he also is free to keep silent. (Note that Figures 2.1 and 2.2 cannot both lay out his problem, for he can't be free to keep silent and also obliged, as in Figure 2.1, to talk.)

Where does this leave Jill? Recall that her options are *S* and *T*, not *A* and *O*; *A* and *O* are actions, *doings*, she can't now think are up to her. (An option of Jill's is some possible action that she thinks is up to her; and, not knowing what Jack will do, she can't believe it is up to her whether, say, she will act as he will.) In Figure 2.2 we have not a game but a one-person decision problem, a problem just for Jack. But if Jill is thinking like Jack, she too partitions in *A*/*O* terms, and she too is facing a problem of the Figure 2.2 sort. (She is the row-chooser there.) She too has no dominant option, and she too need not confess.

Are these people in a Prisoners' Dilemma? If they both put their situation as in Figure 2.1, they are. Not so if they put it as in Figure 2.2 (even if only one of them does). Their being in a Prisoners' Dilemma depends not just on their preferences and beliefs but also on how they *organize* things, on how each agent, as the row-chooser, sets up the columns in his decision matrix. This in turn reflects how each partitions the contingency field he is facing, whether he does that *S*/*T*-wise or *A*/*O*-wise (or otherwise still) – how he *sees* or *understands* what the other might do. We are told what these people believe: the DA said *x*, so they believe *x*. We are told their preferences: each prefers a shorter sentence to a longer. We are not told how they partition. So we can't tell whether the prisoners are in fact in a Dilemma.

Still, this leaves us something worth stressing. If they partition *A/O*-wise (even if only one of them does), they are not in a Dilemma. And since they *may* partition so, since logic alone cannot fault that, logic then leaves them unconstrained. It leaves them each free to keep silent. They are then jointly free to avoid the Pareto-suboptimal (ten-years-each-in-jail) outcome. They might even cooperate, *both* of them keeping silent.

This defeats the DA. It also wards off the social analysts who see a Dilemma in every corner. There may be many fewer Dilemmas than these people think, and fewer bars to cooperation. There may be even fewer if we allow for quasi-*A/O*'ing in many-person cases.[1]

All the above (as also what follows) rests on the common assumption that each party supposes the other's doings (as he puts them) independent of his (her) own, *probabilistically* independent. What if this assumption were dropped? Say that the probability set by Jack on Jill's keeping silent if he keeps silent were allowed to be greater than that of her keeping silent if he talks, that it might be so much greater that the expected utility of his silence would exceed that of his talking. Then Jack would in some cases have to keep silent. Where dependencies are allowed, the thesis that rational prisoners always must talk (must confess) is false.[2] But must they talk in the more common situation, in which there are no dependencies? I am saying that, even there, rationality may let them keep silent, that it lets them keep silent if they don't *S/T*.

2

Here are some likely critiques. First, it may be noted that the prisoners' model has been applied to nonhumans too, to interactions among lower animals, even to some on the bacterial level.[3] No one supposes that, on those levels, the interactors *see* things somehow, that their behavior comports with how they partition the possibilities, that it reflects the *S/T*'ing or *A/O*'ing of their contingency fields. If their being in a Dilemma doesn't depend on their being *S/T*'ers, why does Jack and Jill's being in a Dilemma depend on *their* being *S/T*'ers?

The interactions to which this refers are not Dilemmas at all. They are cases in which two parties meet each other many times over, the interests of each in any single meeting reflecting the matrix in Figure 2.1. The sequence of such meetings is called an *iterated* Dilemma, but it isn't itself a Dilemma. And neither, in the nonhuman cases, are the separate meetings ever separate Dilemmas, for the (nonhuman) parties in them never decide on what to do by reflecting on what the other might do. Bacteria neither reflect nor decide; they only react (or don't) to what their host did just before. Dilemmas are decision problems, and there is no decision problem for nonhumans in an iterated Dilemma. What I am saying about partitioning in a Dilemma therefore doesn't carry over. Conversely, what holds for bacteria needn't hold for Jack and Jill: the fact that a bacterium doesn't *S/T* in any of its interactions has no bearing on whether people can be in a Dilemma without *S/T*'ing.

A second critique faults my view of *A/O*'ing. It holds that *A/O*'ing doesn't exhaust the possibilities that Jack must consider. Besides Jill's doing the same as Jack and her doing the opposite, she might stay silent regardless of what he does and might also talk regardless. Jack's two options and these four possibilities give him a two-*by-four* matrix. In that, there is no dominance either, but his talking when Jill talks regardless is an equilibrium outcome – it is the only such outcome. So, on the usual game analysis, if he is rational, he will talk even here.

This would be right if Jack believed that *A* and *O* were options for Jill, that each was an action she thought up to her. If she now expected to know what Jack will do before she chose, responding in kind and responding conversely would indeed be options for her, and silence regardless and talking regardless would be options too. But he knows she doesn't expect to have this advance information, and that she therefore doesn't think that *A* and *O* are up to her. In his eyes, given what he knows, *A* and *O* are not options for Jill. They remain what she might *do*, and, as *doings*, they are fully exhaustive. She will do one or the other; their disjunction leaves nothing out. (A closely related scenario: Suppose I want to meet you tonight and am debating whether to go to Henry's place or to Niko's to find you. Knowing you never go anywhere else, I take it you either will go to the place to which I will or to the other. What am I leaving out?)[4]

A third critique holds that a rational person has to talk even if he *A*/*O*'s. We will have to pause here a bit to speak about uncertainty.

The cases both of Figure 2.1 and Figure 2.2 are under uncertainty: in neither does either party set any point-probabilities on what the other might do.[5] Some may hold that the probabilities are there, that they just aren't known, aren't known by the agent, that uncertainty is a sort of deficiency of self-knowledge. But let us think of uncertainty instead in terms of probability *ranges*. Let us say that, though people don't always set point-probabilities, they set a probability range – an *at-least-this-and-at-most-that* – on every proposition they entertain, a range whose width may extend from 0 (in cases of risk) to 1 (in total uncertainty). (The cases we are discussing here are under *total* uncertainty.)

This allows for a generalization of expected utility logic. We can say that every option has one or more expected utilities, *one* where the pertinent ranges are zero, *more* where they are wider. In the former situation (risk), the usual logic applies. In the latter (uncertainty), every point selection from the probability ranges – every constriction of them to points – cuts the *many* down to *one*.[6] Every such selection sets up an expected utility for each option, and we can say that a rational person chooses an option whose expected utility, on some point-probability selection, is at least as great as that of any other on the same selection – that he is free to choose any such option.[7]

The problem now seems to be this. Any point-probability selection for the entries in the rows of Figure 2.1 (for the outcomes to which they refer) is a selection for the entries in the same rows of Figure 2.2. This is because the two first rows are the same and row 2 of Figure 2.2 is a permutation of row 2 of Figure 2.1. So the expected utilities are the same too in the two figures; and since that of *T* (the same in both figures) exceeds that of *S* in Figure 2.1, it also exceeds that of *S* in Figure 2.2. In both situations, if both parties are rational, both of them must talk; it makes no difference how they partition.

But note that Jack and Jill are never in both situations, in both Figures 2.1 and 2.2. Each of them partitions *S/T*-wise or *A/O*-wise (or otherwise still) – in just *one* of these ways. And how each partitions determines the figure that lays out his (her) choice problem. It determines which of these figures we then say he (she) *is in*. Note also that a point-selection doesn't select any probabilities for an agent. By assumption, there aren't any: his problem is under uncertainty. It only selects probability stand-ins he might now use in his thinking, in his expected-utility thinking in his current situation. ("Point-probability selection" is short for "selection of point-probability stand-ins.")

The stand-ins he might use in his thinking in some situation he might now be in sometimes wouldn't be usable for him in his now-actual situation. Recall that we assume he supposes the other's doings to be independent of his own, independent of his own doings however he (the agent) partitions the field of the contingencies he is facing. What exactly is this assumption – what is it in the context of uncertainty? It is that, in every problem his partitioning establishes, the agent confines himself to point-selections from his probability ranges that assign to each entry in column 1 the same probability in both rows, and likewise in column 2.[8] This may restrict the agent to different selections under different partitions. It may call for different selections where he *S/T*'s and where he *A/O*'s.

Thus if a selection in a Figure 2.1 case would accord with independence, it would typically fail to accord with independence in a Figure 2.2 case. Row 2 of Figure 2.2 is a permutation of row 2 of Figure 2.1; this means that any selection of the same probability stand-in for each entry in, say, column 1 of Figure 2.1 (in keeping with independence in an *S/T* problem) would as a rule assign *different* stand-ins to the entries in column 1 of Figure 2.2.[9] That being excluded (by independence) for a person in Figure 2.2, he can't there admit these stand-ins, though he could have admitted them were he in Figure 2.1. And he can't admit the (stand-in) *expected* utilities he could have admitted in Figure 2.1. It follows that a person needn't always act the same in both situations – or rather (since he can't *be* in both), that he needn't act in either as he might have were he in the other.

We saw at the start that the dominance of an option isn't immune to matrix transformations, that a matrix in which an option is dominant can be transformed into one in which it isn't. Such a transformation always is possible,[10] but I am saying it only makes sense where a partitioning changes, where the agent changes his view of his contingency field, where he carves that up differently – that it makes sense only where his (subjective) situation changes. Better, forget about transformations: the point is that how he sees that field determines, in part, what his choice problem is and so which matrix is operative for him. Whether he is *S/T*'ing or *A/O*'ing can thus indeed make a difference.

Yet another critique may be offered. This too holds that a rational person has to talk even if he *A/O*'s. It holds that where the expected utilities leave several options open for him, Jack will maximin from them – that he will settle on one of those options the worst (for him) of whose possible outcomes is no worse than the worst possible outcome of any other still-open option. Say that Jack is *A/O*'ing. He is then in Figure 2.2 and both *S* and *T* remain open. The worst of the outcomes of *T* is better than the worst outcome of *S*. Jack will therefore take *T*.

I will here be very brief. I find no merit in this. A person who maximins takes an option (or one of those options) whose worst possible outcome is no worse than that of any other. He does this even where, if that followed, he would wish he had done something else and he knows this beforehand. (In Figure 2.2, he takes *T*, since *T,A* is the maximin outcome, though he knows that, if *T,A* followed, he would wish he had taken *S*.) He sees each option in terms of what would be worst for him if he took it, keeping himself focused always on his faring as badly as he might. His policy isn't just pessimistic: act on the worst-case contingency, act as if that were true. (*Is* there a worst-case contingency where he is *A/O*'ing?) It is close to neurotic: act as if whatever you did would turn out as badly as it could.[11] Jack is free to follow this line, but logic doesn't require him to. If he is rational, he needn't take *T*. That is, unless he *S/T*'s – how he partitions *can* make a difference.

3

That how, as the agents involved, we partition can make a difference has been noted before. Recall Nelson Goodman's *blue/green – grue/bleen* pair of color partitions. Goodman wasn't speaking of choices but of prediction and inference. Still, my point is very like his.

A hundred marbles, all of them blue, have been drawn from an urn; the next to be drawn (tomorrow morning) will very likely be blue. The marbles drawn also were *bleen*, a bleen one being one that is drawn before this coming midnight and is blue or is drawn just then or after and is green – for *grue*, switch "blue" and "green" in this. Parity of logic implies that the next marble is likely to be bleen; and since that marble will be drawn tomorrow, this says it is likely to be green, *not* blue.

The self-same evidence, differently put (in *blue/green* terms or in *grue/bleen* terms), sometimes yields conflicting predictions. Again, how we partition can make a difference.[12]

Which partition should we then use? In Goodman's case, this may be thought clear. We want to make correct predictions about what will happen tomorrow, and *blue/green*'ing would help us to do that and *grue/bleen*'ing wouldn't, or so at least we believe (never mind on what grounds we believe it). So we reject the *grue/bleen* partition.[13] Is there any similar basis for rejecting either *S/T*'ing or *A/O*'ing? Is there something we want to do that one or the other would keep us from doing?

Suppose we are Jack and want to make sure we avoid sure-thing regrets, regrets we would have whichever option Jill took – call this desire *d*. *A/O*'ing would keep us from satisfying *d*, for *A/O*'ing would let us take *S*, which we would regret having done whether Jill took *S* or *T* (and only these two are her *options*). Or suppose we want to avoid being obliged to act in a way that would make for a Pareto-suboptimum if Jill acted likewise – call this desire *d'*. *S/T*'ing would keep us from satisfying *d'*, for *S/T*'ing would have us take *T*, and *T,T* is Pareto-suboptimal. *d* would exclude *A/O*'ing for us, and *d'* would exclude *S/T*'ing. But *d* attends to what would happen if Jill took *S* or took *T*, and *d'* attends to what would happen if she did as we did or the opposite: a *d*-terms analysis resorts to *S/T*'ing and a *d'*-analysis to *A/O*'ing. Each of them excludes one partition by making use of the other. That sort of exclusion only begs the question.

Consider also desire *d''*, the desire to avoid being obliged to act in a way that would make for a Pareto-suboptimum *if Jill took T*. (*d''* is like *d'* except for its last clause.) This too would exclude *S/T*'ing. But here we are thinking of what would happen *if Jill took T*, which makes use of the *S/T* partition. A *d''*-analysis excludes *S/T*'ing by resorting to it, and such exclusions discredit themselves. Neither *d* nor *d'* nor *d''* does the job it is meant to do, and I can think of no other likely candidates for that job.

Here is a second approach to the problem. Some partitions are parasitic; they live off the concepts of others. Say that two partitions conflict, that applying some logic we have to each in turn would yield different judgments. If one partition is conceptually prior to the other, that may be the one we should use. Goodman takes up this idea, and he notes that it doesn't help him.

One partition is prior to another if that other can be defined in its terms (plus perhaps some independent matters) and the reverse doesn't hold. Let B be that marble x is blue, let G be that it is green, let G^{∇} be that it is grue, and let B^{∇} be that it is bleen. Let $M-$ be that x will be drawn before midnight and $M+$ that it will be drawn at midnight or after. $G^{\nabla} \vee B^{\nabla}$ can be put in the terms of B and G (and $M-$ and $M+$), as in

(1) $(M- \cdot G \vee M+ \cdot B) \vee (M- \cdot B \vee M+ \cdot G)$

But this can be reversed: $B \vee G$ can be put in the terms of G^{∇} and B^{∇} (and $M-$ and $M+$), as in

(2) $(M- \cdot B^{\nabla} \vee M+ \cdot G^{\nabla}) \vee (M- \cdot G^{\nabla} \vee M+ \cdot B^{\nabla})$

So neither of these partitions is conceptually prior to the other.

Likewise for our partitions here. Let the subscripts "k" and "l" stand for Jack and Jill. $A_l \vee O_l$ can be put in the terms of S_l and T_l (and S_k and T_k), as in

(3) $(S_k \cdot S_l \vee T_k \cdot T_l) \vee (S_k \cdot T_l \vee T_k \cdot S_l)$

And $S_l \vee T_l$ can be put in the terms of A_l and O_l (and S_k and T_k), as in

(4) $(S_k \cdot A_l \vee T_k \cdot O_l) \vee (S_k \cdot O_l \vee T_k \cdot A_l)$

S/T and *A/O* – like *B/G* and G^{∇}/B^{∇} – can each be defined in the terms of the other. Neither can claim priority on either pragmatic or definitional grounds. This means that neither can be favored (or excluded) on either sort of grounds.

What about *epistemic* priority? Whatever we have to do to learn whether a marble is blue or green, we have to do more to learn whether that marble is grue or bleen: we have to determine when it was drawn. So too, whatever we have to do to learn whether Jill is silent or talking, we have to do more to discover whether she is doing what Jack is or the opposite: we have to determine what Jack is doing. This is not wholly beyond dispute,[14] but suppose we let it pass. Why should the epistemic priority of one partition over another oblige us to favor the former? What if someone favored the epistemically *less*-basic partition, the one we need more data to use, on the grounds of that fuller data's being the more informative? Neither of these favoring biases has more credit than the other.

4

Let us move back a step. The prisoners in their separate cells may be unclear as to where they stand. They know which choice pairs would lead to which outcomes – the DA told them this. Both of them know how each ranks these outcomes. But it may be that one or the other hasn't yet settled on how to map the contingencies he (she) is facing, hasn't yet partitioned the field. We need a name for this situation – call it the Prisoners' *Plight*. I have argued that not all people in a Plight are in a Dilemma.

More fully, in a Prisoners' Plight, all the following holds. Each of the parties (in our two-person cases) has two options, X and Y – pegged to Jack (k) and Jill (l), these are X_k and Y_k and X_l and Y_l. There is no fellow-feeling between them or expectation of future meetings. They rank the outcomes of their jointly taking their options as in Figure 2.3. For Jack, Y_k is dominant; for Jill, Y_l is dominant. The case is one of uncertainty (no probabilities for either), but each supposes that what the other will do is independent of what *he* will do. And they both are aware of all this.[15] I will refer to it all together as their being *in Figure 2.3*.

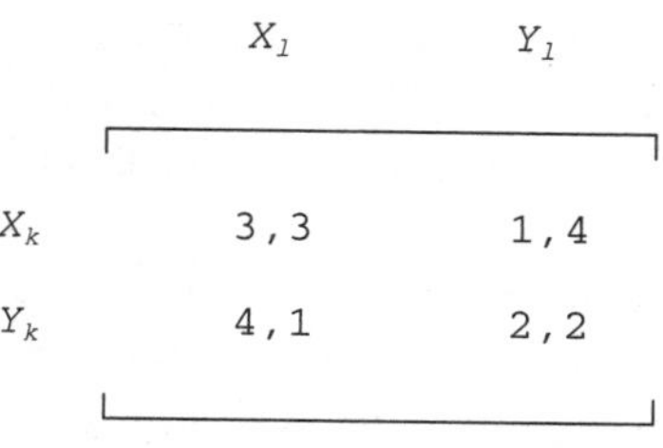

	X_1	Y_1
X_k	3,3	1,4
Y_k	4,1	2,2

Figure 2.3

Call the matrix in this figure Jack and Jill's *option* matrix. It shows only Jack and Jill's options and how each ranks the different outcomes of their each taking some option they have. It doesn't lay out all the factors on which, in the end, they will choose. It is formally like the matrix in Figure 2.1, but that matrix is a *decision* matrix, one that also shows how the parties partition their contingency fields. Jack and Jill are in a Prisoners' Plight where they are in Figure 2.3, where that figure presents what they know of their own and the other's options and their pertinent preferences. They are in a Prisoners' Dilemma where, besides, they are in a game, where each not only knows that the other has certain options to choose from but sees the other as now preparing to make a choice from among them – they are there in Figure 2.3 and also in Figure 2.1. Where they are in Figure 2.3 and their decision matrix (as the row-chooser), or that of just one of them, is like that in Figure 2.2, they are in a Plight but not in a Dilemma.[16]

In the vast literature on this subject, it is always taken for granted that people in a Plight are in a Dilemma. This amounts to supposing that people in a Figure 2.3 situation always see their contingency field as a disjunction of the other's options – in the case of the prisoners, as *Either S or T*. It amounts to supposing that every Figure 2.3 case is a Figure 2.1 case. I have suggested that the prisoners sometimes see their contingency field as in Figure 2.2: as *Either A or O*. They are not then in a Dilemma and they sometimes reject the option that is dominant in their option matrix. Why is it held that rational people in a Plight never do this, that they always see the contingencies in the *S or T* way, that they are always in a Dilemma and so always choose *T*?

Those who take this line are economists or at least students of economics, which raises the possibility that their special orientation predisposes them to it. People versed in economics think of the agents in an exchange economy – the producers, the buyers, the sellers – as governing the choices they make by the choices the others involved might make, by the *options* these others have. Von Neumann and Morgenstern are explicit about this. They contrast the decision making of a person alone in his world (Robinson Crusoe on his island) with that of a person in a setting of others:

> Not a single datum with which he [Crusoe] has to deal reflects another person's will or intention. . . . A participant in a social exchange economy, on the other hand, faces data of this last type as well: they are the product of other participants' actions and volitions (like prices). His actions will be influenced by his expectations of these, and they in turn reflect the other participants' expectation of his actions.[17]

This overstates it a bit. A person in an exchange economy *knows* what the others might choose to do, but that needn't enter his thinking. He needn't think in terms of the others' choosing and acting on their options, in terms of their "volitions" – he might present what they could do as actions that aren't option-takings (as in Figure 2.2). Still, he does often think in these terms, and perhaps he should be called an *economic* agent only where he does. In many studies in economics, such thinking indeed defines a person's being an economic agent, such an agent being one of a number of interactors each of whom thinks of (*sees*) the others as choosing and acting on some options they have. The project of economics, of *micro*economics, is to study economic agency, and those who work in economics have thus been primed to think of people as thinking of others that way. Where they speak of people in a Plight, they then consider them in a Dilemma. And so do the many other writers whom economic theory has influenced.

In arguing that Plights need not be Dilemmas, my purpose was to suggest that they sometimes *aren't*. This would mean that people sometimes aren't economic agents, that they don't always *S/T*, that they are not always playing games (of the game-theory sort). I cannot prove this suggestion, but it would be very surprising if it weren't true. For just as economists are primed by their theory to think of people as always *S/T*'ers, so we all (economists included) are prompted to be *A/O*'ers.

There is nothing subtle in this widespread pattern of prompting. From early childhood, we are urged to reflect on what would happen if everyone acted as we do. A bright child says, "They won't!", and that may be the way to respond in the usual many-person case. In our two-person cases, there is often no basis for saying that the other won't act as we will, and, in such cases, the old admonition sometimes resonates with us. There are many variants of it. In some, it is meant to settle things. But often it is only meant to bring out one consideration. A second consideration (in a two-options-each case) is what would happen if the other person did the opposite.[18] Attending to both possibilities – letting their disjunction shape our problem – sets up an *A/O* case.

Some people in a Plight are moved by the admonition. Others put it out of mind. Those who are moved are then *A/O*'ers, at least in the case at hand. They are not in a Dilemma. The others may well be *S/T*'ers, in which case their Plights are Dilemmas. Who is moved and who isn't? I have no answer, but this may be true, that those who hold a general theory about what people are like, who think that the *natural* way to be, are themselves drawn to being that way. That would provide for this conjecture, that theorists committed to economics, who think of people as economic agents and so as being *S/T*'ers,

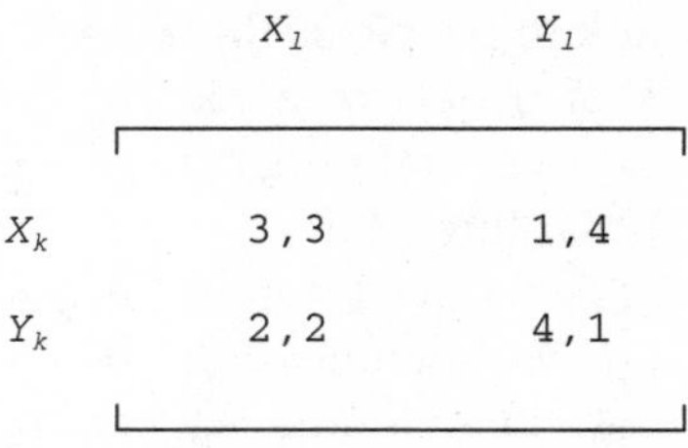

Figure 2.4

are themselves more likely to be *S/T'*ers than others. It would follow that economists in a Plight are more often in a Dilemma than others, that they more often try to free-ride than do other people. There is some evidence that this is so,[19] but we had better leave that open.

5

A word about my title question. All the above had to do with Plights. But just as not all Plights are Dilemmas, so not every Dilemma is a Plight. The option matrix in Figure 2.4 is not that of a Plight; there are no dominant options in it that might make for a Pareto-suboptimum. Let Jack and Jill be in Figure 2.4. If they both are *S/T'*ers, their *decision* matrix is the one in Figure 2.2: they are not in a Dilemma. If they are *A/O'*ers, each has as his (her) decision matrix the matrix in Figure 2.1. Though they then are not in a game, they *are* in a Dilemma – if they both act rationally, they will wish they both hadn't. This reverses what we noted about *S/T'*ing and *A/O'*ing in Plights.

So we cannot generalize about who suffers from Dilemmas, only about what makes for Dilemmas where people are in a Plight. Still, we may not need any more. Plights have always been common. That says something about the human condition (a vexing question: what *does* it say?), and it makes them worth studying. The situation in Figure 2.4 has no such special significance.

3

HAVING, GAINING, LOSING

ECONOMISTS have sometimes noted that we don't always value situations just by what we would have in them. They note that our thinking often instead looks to our gains or losses, to how what we might come to have differs from what we currently have. This, they hold, speaks badly for us, since the usual sorts of such thinking run against the logic of value. I argue that they don't run against it, and that giving such thinking its due lets us clear up a number of issues.

1

Here is a much-discussed concept, that of *endowment effects*. Richard Thaler, who introduced the idea, speaks of "the underweighting of opportunity costs" relative to out-of-pocket expenses.[1] Kahneman, Knetsch, and Thaler speak of "the increased value of a good to an individual when the good becomes part of the individual's endowment."[2] Tversky and Kahneman note that "the loss of utility associated with giving up a valued good is greater than the utility gain associated with receiving it."[3]

I will put it this way, that where we have something we value, losing it often matters more to us than gaining it would have mattered if we didn't have it. We insist on getting more for giving up that something than we would have paid for it if we didn't have it. Thaler offers this example: "Mr. R bought a case of good wine in the late 50s for about $5 a bottle. A few years later his wine merchant offered to buy the wine back for $100 a bottle. He refused, although he has never paid more than $35 for a bottle of wine"[4] (and would presumably not have paid more on the day he refused to sell for $100).

The point is that something's now being *ours* is itself often value-affective. It leads us to value that something more highly than we would if we didn't now have it. The "something" this speaks of might be anything valued. It might be some physical object or some quantity of some good (Mr. R's case of wine). It might be a right or entitlement, or a chance we have of some benefit, or a mere probabilistic advantage. Thaler speaks of a study he made of the value people put on their lives. He asked people how large a payment would get them to accept an extra .001 risk of immediate death, and he asked also what they would pay (if the risk were greater by .001 than in fact it was) to reduce their risk of death by the same amount. He reports that a typical answer was "I wouldn't pay more than $200, but I wouldn't accept the extra risk for $50,000!"[5]

Some writers make use of a related idea. They speak of issues in which one option is a status-quo option – our staying in place, our making no change. In an issue of such a sort, we sometimes value that option more highly than we would were our options the same but one of the others the status quo. To put it in terms of choosing, let our options be A and B, the status-quo option being B: we sometimes choose B though we would have chosen A were that the status-quo option. This favoring of the status quo is what Samuelson and Zeckhauser call the *status quo bias*.[6]

They discuss many instances. Here is one close to home. American professors can allocate the funds in their retirement accounts in different proportions to TIAA (bonds) and to CREF (mostly stocks). The returns on these investments differ over time, but many professors ignore the returns and keep to their initial allocations, whatever they were – they keep to their status quos. Another instance: when the "new" Coke came out, most Coke drinkers didn't switch, though in blind testing many preferred the "new" Coke to the "old." They would probably have stayed with "new" Coke had they been drinking that.

The authors offer some explanations of this common bias. First, there may be transition costs, and these may deter us from changing. (There are no costs attached to changing TIAA/CREF allocations, nor to switching from "old" to "new" Coke.) Also, we often try to keep a good opinion of ourselves. Turning away from a status quo that we ourselves have established may lead to self-censure, which we want to avoid. (This may apply in the TIAA/CREF case but not in that of the Cokes.) They also refer to Kahneman and Tversky's (and others') concept of *loss aversion*.[7] That is perhaps the fundamental concept.

The thesis of loss aversion is this, that a loss of some amount of some good usually matters more to us than would a gain of the same amount – that "losses loom larger than gains." Notice that both endowment effects and loss aversion involve disparities of disvalues/values but that the disparities are of different sorts. In an endowment effect, the disparity is between the disvalues/values we set on losing some quantity x' of some good and on gaining-it-*if-we-didn't-have-it*; the former at our status-quo point, where we have $x'' + x'$, the latter at the point at which we would be *if we had only* x''.[8] In a case of loss aversion, the disparity is between the disvalues/values we set on losing x' and on gaining-x'-*in-addition-to-all-we-now-have* (that is, on top of $x'' + x'$) – only one basing point there, the one at which we have $x'' + x'$.

A sensitivity to both gains and losses typically diminishes with their size; that is, increasingly larger gains/losses are assigned diminishingly greater value/disvalue. A typical gains/losses value curve thus has the shape of a sloping *S* with its point of inflection (a kink) at the status-quo point. (Loss aversion appears in its being steeper for losses than for gains at equal distances from that point.) Kahneman and Tversky draw such a curve as in Figure 3.1a. The curve in Figure 3.1b

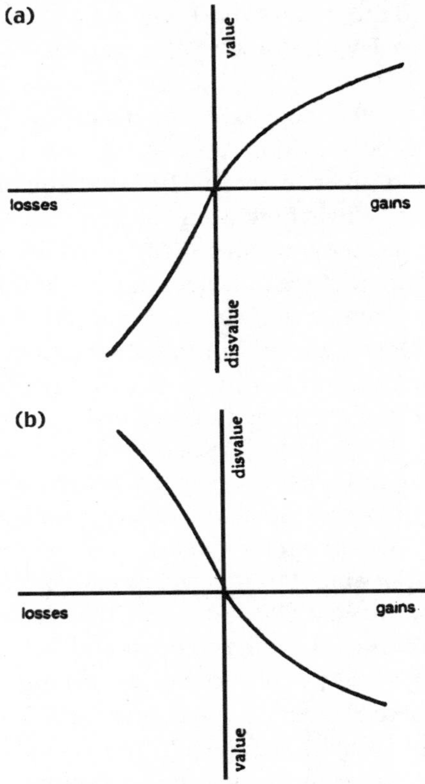

Figure 3.1

exhibits the same, the sign of the vertical axis only being the reverse of that in Figure 3.1a, the disvalue of possible losses being plotted *above* the intersection, the value of possible gains *below*. We will find it convenient to refer to Figure 3.1b in what follows.

Tversky and Kahneman themselves take loss aversion to be basic. They say it explains both endowment effects and the status-quo bias. Speaking of endowment effects, they describe them as "an immediate consequence of loss aversion."[9]

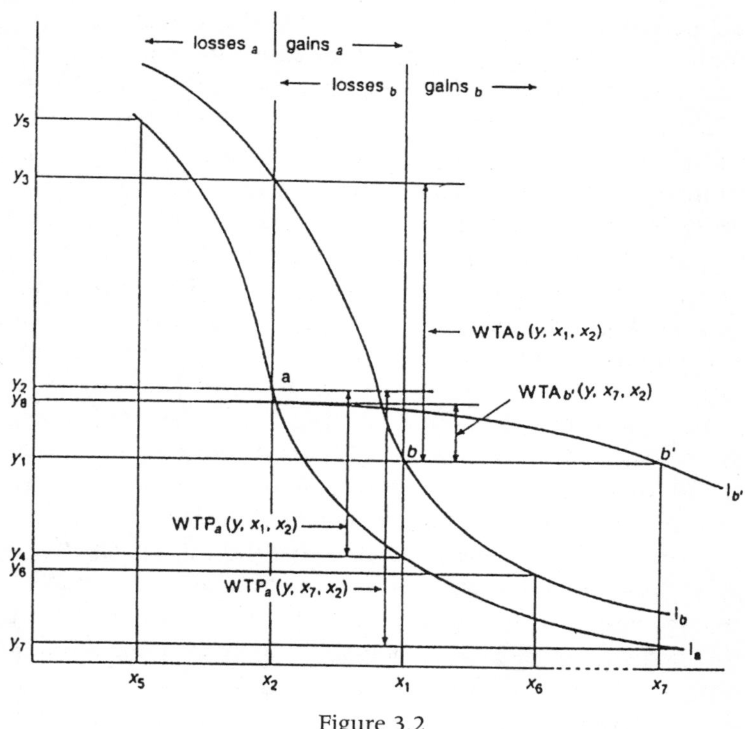

Figure 3.2

Are they *always* a consequence? How are all these concepts related? This calls for some further analysis of them.

2

Think of cases in which the possible endowments are positive quantities of x and of y. Let the agent be at b in Figure 3.2, at which point he has x_1, y_1. Above that point, the curve through b maps the least amount of y (over y_1) that the agent at b would accept as compensation for different losses of x (from x_1). *Below* that point, it maps the most of y (below y_1) he would be willing to yield, to *pay*, to gain different amounts of x (over x_1).[10] Were this person at *a*, he would have $x_2,y_2 - x_2 < x_1$ and $y_2 > y_1$. The curve through *a* is like the one through *b* but speaks of losses and gains of *x* from or above what he would have at *a*.

These two curves are indifference curves, though not of the usual sort. They connect possible gains and losses from their basing points *b* and *a*, possible gains and losses of *x*. The curve through *b* – call it I_b – shows that the agent at *b* is indifferent between staying at *b* and moving for a gain from *b* (a gain_b) to x_6,y_6 and indifferent also between both of these options and moving for a loss from *b* to x_2,y_3 – and between these and various other smaller and larger moves. Correspondingly for I_a.

Being gain/loss indifference curves, the curves exhibit loss aversion. (As in Figure 3.1b, whose axis-intersection corresponds to *b* and to *a*, the thresholds of both gaining and losing on I_b and I_a.)[11] Does our having such indifference curves mean that there are endowment effects – that there are such effects at, say, *b* – that our losing something at *b* matters more to us than gaining it would have mattered if we didn't have it? Let the "something" be $x_1 - x_2$. The question needs some pinning down, for what *would* we have had if we didn't have this "something"? Perhaps we would have had x_2,y_1, having then as much of *y* as we have at *b*, but perhaps we would have had more (or less) than y_1 of *y*. Say that we just bought $x_1 - x_2$ for $y_2 - y_1$; if we hadn't bought it, we would now have x_2,y_2. I will let what we would have had be x_2,y_2 – our would-have-had point will be *a*. This won't affect the analysis. (The would-have-had point could be other than *a*, but then some changing of the curves would be needed, some flattening or steepening of them.)

Let $\text{WTA}_b(y,x_1,x_2)$ be the least amount of *y* we would at *b* be *willing to accept* as compensation for losing $x_1 - x_2$. Let $\text{WTP}_a(y,x_1,x_2)$ be the most of *y* we would at *a* be *willing to pay* to gain $x_1 - x_2$. Our question about endowment effects is whether loss aversion makes for $\text{WTA}_b(y,x_1,x_2) > \text{WTP}_a(y,x_1,x_2)$.[12] In Figure 3.2, the answer is *yes*; but, in general, it depends on the curves, on their relation to each other, which may in turn depend on the difference in x between b and a, on $x_1 - x_2$.

In the simplest situation, the loss-part of I_b is exactly like that of I_a – for every loss of x we would want the same y-compensation at b and at a. In such cases, if $(x_1 - x_2) = (x_2 - x_5)$, then $(y_3 - y_1) = (y_5 - y_2)$. Since, by loss aversion, $(y_5 - y_2) > (y_2 - y_4)$, we here have $(y_3 - y_1) > (y_2 - y_4)$, which means that $WTA_b(y,x_1,x_2) > WTP_a(y,x_1,x_2)$, an endowment effect. So where the *loss* parts of the curves are congruent, loss aversion makes for endowment effects. And likewise where the *gain* parts of these curves are congruent.

Often neither the loss parts nor the gain parts of the curves are congruent. Indeed, it is likely that the more of x we have, the amount of y remaining the same, the flatter our gain/loss curve through our status-quo point – a principle of diminishing *marginal* sensitivity. (The more of, say, land we have, all else remaining the same, the less we will accept for losing x' acres and the less we will pay to get x' more.)[13] Still, where the amount of x in b isn't much greater than that in a, I_b and I_a don't differ much (or so I will suppose). They are then close to being congruent, and the situation approximates that in the paragraph just above. So we come to this, that loss aversion makes for endowment effects where $x_1 - x_2$ is small.[14]

It is a surprising corollary of diminishing marginal sensitivity that, where $x_1 - x_2$ is *large*, there may be a converse effect. Suppose we were at b' in Figure 3.2 and that $x_7 - x_2$ is large – this is like supposing $x_1 - x_2$ to be large. Let a be our would-have-had point if we didn't have $x_7 - x_2$. Since at b' we have much more of x than we would have at a (say, a much larger amount of land), our gain/loss curve might be $I_{b'}$, a curve much flatter than I_a. (The curves would cross; we will get to that.) Here $y_2 - y_7$ would be greater than $y_8 - y_1$. That is, the loss of $x_7 - x_2$ would matter to us *less* than gaining it would have mattered if we didn't have it, and so $WTA_{b'}(y,x_7,x_2) < WTP_a(y,x_7,x_2)$, a *converse* endowment effect. (We would accept less for $x_7 - x_2$ acres than we would have paid for them if we didn't have them!) That there may be some such cases is implicit in our assumptions. Still, it would be nice to find a real-life converse effect.[15]

Notice that there being such cases squares with the thesis of loss aversion. Losses "loom larger" than gains (loss aversion) where both losses and gains are counted from the same basing point. They needn't loom larger where, as here, the loss is from b' and the gain is from a. Loss aversion itself implies no endowment effects, direct or converse.[16] It does make for endowment effects proper where $x_1 - x_2$ is small. And it allows for converse effects where $x_1 - x_2$ is large.

Now for the status-quo bias. Since the agent at b in Figure 3.2 wants more than $y_2 - y_1$ in exchange for $x_1 - x_2$, he will refuse to move to a. So we can say he prefers b to a. We could say he has the opposite preference if he wanted *less* than $y_2 - y_1$. In terms of I_b, a person at b prefers b to a if his I_b passes above a, and he prefers a to b if it passes *below* a. (This will soon be modified slightly.) Or think of him at a: since he would pay more than $y_2 - y_1$ in order to gain $x_1 - x_2$, he would there prefer b to a, and he would have the opposite preference if he would only pay less than that. The agent is at b, and his I_b in Figure 3.2 shows that he prefers b to a. His I_a shows that, were he at a, he would have the same preference. Being at b, he chooses b, and at a he would choose the same. No status-quo bias here.

But look now at Figure 3.3. Here I_a and I_b are such that $y_4 > y_1$ – that is, I_a here passes above b. This means that, were the agent at a, he would pay *less* than $y_2 - y_1$ in order to gain $x_1 - x_2$. He would at a prefer a to b. He is (we assume) at b, and his I_b passes above a, which reveals his preference now for b over a. Being at b, he chooses b, but were he at a, he would choose a. At either point, he would keep what he had. Here we encounter a status-quo bias.

In sum, where $x_1 - x_2$ is small, loss aversion yields endowment effects,[17] and these yield a status-quo bias where $y_4 > y_1$

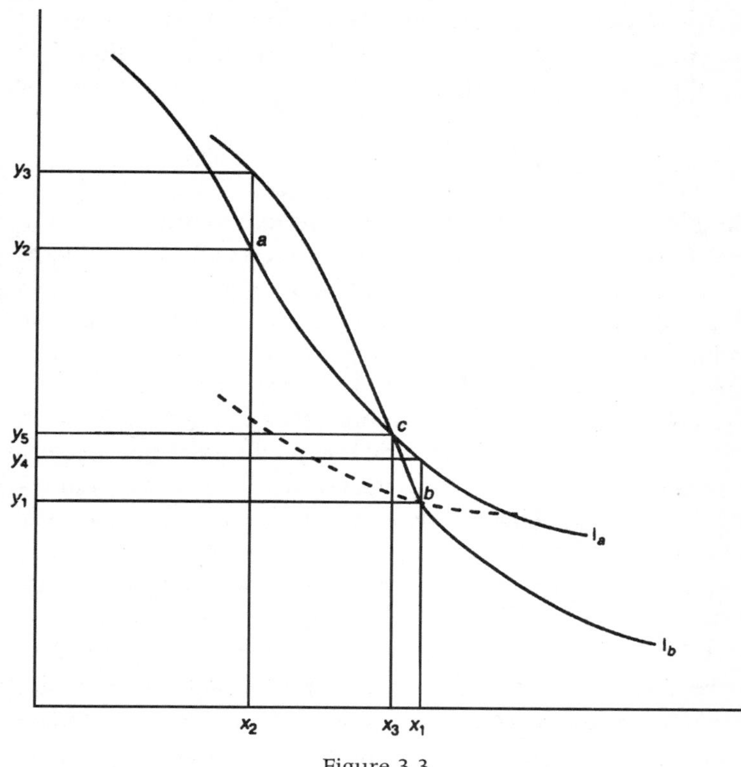

Figure 3.3

and $WTA_b(y,x_1,x_2)$ is sufficiently larger than $WTP_a(y,x_1,x_2)$ – where it still is that $y_3 > y_2$. Loss aversion doesn't always yield a status-quo bias, but it does yield such a bias in certain special cases.

There may sometimes also be a *converse* bias here. Look again at Figure 3.2 and suppose that the agent is at b'; let $x_7 - x_2$ be large. His $I_{b'}$ passes below a, which means he prefers a to b'. But were this person at a, he would prefer b' to a (his I_a passes below b'). Being at b', he chooses a, though at a he would choose b'. Here is a converse status-quo bias: at whichever point he was, this person would opt for the other, the one that *wasn't* his status quo.[18] Again, we must allow for this, but finding a real-life case would be nice.

3

Should loss aversion and endowment effects and status-quo bias be faulted? (Let us keep to *non*converse effects and biases only.) Those who write about these matters report them as lapses of logic. But loss aversion just brings out how people value losses and gains; and that enters logic as a *given*, like our utility judgments of risk and of successive increments of a good. Loss aversion thus cannot be faulted any more than can risk aversion or diminishing marginal utility. Endowment effects follow where $x_1 - x_2$ is small, so they too can't be faulted. And since these yield a status-quo bias in certain special cases, we might expect to find such a bias to be untroubling too. Still, what makes these cases special is itself usually thought to cause trouble.

What is special about these cases is that the agent's indifference curves cross. On the usual microeconomic analysis, this can never happen; logic is shown to rule it out. Thus that analysis cannot credit any status-quo bias. Indeed, that analysis can't even credit all endowment effects, for sometimes these too (as in Figure 3.3) involve a crossing of curves.

Here is the usual argument against indifference curves crossing. (The curves of the usual sort are convex, but that plays no role in this.) Rational indifference is transitive. In Figure 3.3, I_a and I_b cross at *c*; the agent is indifferent between *a* and *c* and between *c* and *b*. But I_b passes above *a*, so the agent prefers *b* to *a*. He *isn't* indifferent between them – transitivity doesn't hold for him. If he is rational, that can't be right, so I_b can't pass above *a*. Neither could it have passed below it, nor above or below any other point on I_a. If the agent is rational, I_b and I_a can't cross.

Tversky and Kahneman offer a way of thinking about curves that do cross.[19] They suggest that every preference has a *reference* point, and that a preference from point *r* needn't agree with any from *s*, and so too with indifferences. More broadly: our *values* are reference-dependent. A value *structure* is a family of reference-point-indexed rankings, one such ranking for every point at which we might now be. All the rankings in our value structure hold for us concurrently, but only one is operative at any particular moment – at any given *location*. All our rankings except for one are thus conditional (counterfactual), the one that isn't being the one indexed by our *present* location. A person at *r* acts on his values indexed by *r*, on his values_r. Were he now at *s*, he would act on his values_s.

If a person is rational, each ranking in his value structure satisfies the usual logic. That logic doesn't apply, however, to all these rankings together, to sets of preferences and indifferences taken from differently indexed rankings. If the agent prefers_a *a* to *b*, he can't prefer_a *b* to *a*, but he *can* prefer_b *b* to *a*. If he prefers_b *b* to *a* and prefers_b *a* to some *d*, he must prefer_b *b* to *d*. But preferring_b *b* to *a* and preferring_a *a* to some *d*, he needn't prefer_b *b* to *d*. So too of course for indifference.

This lets some indifference curves cross. I_a in Figure 3.3 is the agent's indifference_a curve; I_b is his indifference_b curve.[20] The agent is indifferent_a between *a* and *c*, indifferent_b between *c* and *b*, and *not* indifferent_a between *a* and *b*. But this isn't an intransitivity, a lapse of proper entailment, for differently indexed indifferences don't jointly entail any others. Thus the case against the crossing of I_a and I_b doesn't hold. The agent now being at *b*, only the indifferences mapped by I_b are now operative for him; those mapped by I_a are *not* operative. And a person's operative indifferences are logically independent of his nonoperative ones.

What is the purpose of indexing? It lets us say that a rational person might have a status-quo bias, that he might prefer *b* to *a* at *b* but prefer *a* to *b* at *a*.[21] It does that by getting the crossing of I_a and I_b to *not* imply intransitivities. We must now ask what else might do that, and whether it mightn't be done more simply.

Consider this different theory. In place of a set of separate rankings, each of them same-point indexed, think of the agent as having one ranking of all situations *under all possible descriptions*. The indexing theory supposes the existence of different rankings of the same situations, these being the agent's different rankings conditional on his being at *a* or at *b*.... The new theory speaks of a single ranking – a single actual ranking he has. This is a ranking of situations not in their natural, naked state but *under every possible report or description of each.* That means that the objects of preference and indifference are here situations as *described* somehow, that they are *propositions.*

Think of propositions about certain just-incurred gains and losses. These describe *a* and *b* and *c*... in terms of the changes, if any, involved in getting to them from *here* or from *there*. The agent's gain/loss indifference curves – we might have called them his *changes* curves – map his reactions to such propositions. The curves in Figure 3.3 don't show him indifferent between *a* and *c* and between *c* and *b* simpliciter. Rather, I_a shows him indifferent between *p*: *Being at a* (or *I am at a*...) *as a result of no change* and *q*: *Being at c as a result of moving from a* (as a result of gaining $x_3 - x_2$ in exchange for $y_2 - y_5$). And I_b shows him indifferent between *r*: *Being at c as a result of moving from b* (as a result of losing $x_1 - x_3$ and getting $y_5 - y_1$) and *s*: *Being at b as a result of no change.*[22] I_b also reveals his preference for *Being at b as a result of no change* over *Being at a as a result of moving from b.*[23] The objects of each indifference he has, as also of each of his preferences, is a proposition pair – again, he is indifferent between *p* and *q* and between *r* and *s*. Where, as here, two pairs are discrete (no constituents shared), transitivity doesn't apply, and there can't be *in*transitivity.

It turns out we don't need indexing to let gain/loss indifference curves cross. Nor do we need it to allow for the rationality of a status-quo bias. For we can lay out such a bias in terms of discrete proposition-pairs, as, say, a preference for *s* over *t*: for *Being at b as a result of no change* over *Being at a as a result of moving from b* along with another for *p* over *u*: for *Being at a as a result of no change* over *Being at b as a result of moving from a*. Still, these preferences hold for the agent here and now, say at *b*, and a status-quo bias has to do with his preferences at two locations, with those he now has at *b* and those he *would* have at *a*. To allow for a status-quo bias, we must assume a congruence of his actual and conditional preferences, a congruence of his *b*-actual and *a*-conditional preferences focused on propositions referring to *b* and to *a*. We must assume that the so-focused preferences he would have at *a*, were he at that point, are among those he now has at *b* – that his so-focused preferences would be the same at either point. In fact, I believe, this often holds, and so we are free to proceed.

Our gain/loss curves I_a and I_b are not the usual indifference curves, the ones in textbooks of economics. The usual curves connect propositions referring only to what *is had*. They plot the agent's indifferences regarding his having this or that bundle, having those bundles simpliciter: they plot his indifferences regarding certain havings independently of what he had before. Call these curves his *havings* curves. The dashed curve in Figure 3.3 is an instance. This shows the agent indifferent between certain *x,y*-havings alone – his having x_1, y_1 is proposition *m*, his having x_2, y_2 is *n*, etc.[24] His g/l curves connect propositions about *alterations* in havings. These plot his indifferences regarding gains and losses and nonchanges from what he had before: they connect *p* and *q*, and *r* and *s*, etc.[25]

Each of us has preferences and indifferences focusing only on what we might have and others that focus on changes or nonchanges from certain basing points. Our comprehensive value ranking collects all these various valuations. It collects all our havings values (e.g., a preference for *n* over *m*) and our gains-and-losses values (e.g., a preference for *s* over *t*). This just enlarges on the *havings* approach; it does not conflict with it. But it raises the question of which of our valuations enter our thinking – which valuations enter *when*. When do we go by our havings values and when by our gains-and-losses values? What determines which of our values motivate us here and now?

Here is the answer I favor. Any situation can be described in any number of ways. Still, only one description of it reflects our *seeing* or *understanding* of it, and our operative values are those that focus on propositions describing things *as we see them*. The values we have that move us are those wired-up by our seeings, those that our seeings make relevant. Where our havings are salient for us, where we see outcomes as what we would *have*, we wire-up the values we put on the havings involved. Where we see them as gains or losses, we wire-up the values we put on changes from our basing point. And how we choose and act depends on which of our values are wired.

What is a *seeing* of something? I take this up in other places,[26] so I won't do that here. I find no definitions that help – neither of seeings nor of preference or of belief and the like. But no problem in that; we can make do without definitions where we grasp how these concepts are used.

Still, there may be uneasiness. The values that move us are those that we set on propositions describing things as we see them. How then *should* we see things? Logic can bypass this question. Where our concern is with logic only, with what course would be rational for us, our having no answer can't trouble us. What matters in logic is what our premises *are* (our beliefs and preferences and seeings . . .), not what they *ought* to be. We may well be troubled, however, where we ask what course would be *right*.

Suppose we are asking what should be done about economic inequality. Utilitarians sometimes argue that shifting wealth from the rich to the poor would bring about a social gain, at least where all the people involved have the same utility curve for wealth. A utility curve is not an indifference curve. It maps the values set on havings of different amounts of x alone, not on the sameness of value of different amounts of x and y – it has the shape of the curve in the upper-right quadrant of Figure 3.1a. Let x be wealth; Jack Rich has x_1, Jill Poor has x_2. Let $x' = \frac{1}{2}(x_1 - x_2)$. Because of the downward slope of the curve, moving Jack to $x_1 - x'$ and Jill to $x_2 + x'$ would raise the utility level of Jill by more than it lowered that of Jack. The total utility would rise.[27]

This takes a time-slice view. It sees the outcomes solely in terms of what these people would then *have*. Suppose that they themselves see them as gains and losses, and that, at each possible basing point, their g/l curves are congruent.[28] Let $x_1 - x_2$ be small, Jack not much richer than Jill. There are then endowment effects, and losing x' would matter more to Jack than gaining it would matter to Jill.[29] If we went by the values these people put on the outcomes as *they* see them, the case for a redistribution of wealth, for an equalization, would fail.[30] Should we go by how they see them or by how some outsider sees them? It may be that the answer depends on how they *should* be seen. Yes, but how *should* they be seen?

Consider also Ronald Dworkin's (and others') *envy-freeness* test: an allocation of goods (of money and health and...) should be such that no one envies others, such that no one "prefer[s] someone else's bundle... to his own."[31] Does this refer to a preference for a *mere having* of some other's bundle (for now being "in his shoes," however one got to be in them) or to a readiness for *swapping* with him, a preference for changing over staying put? Should we see an allocation in terms of what people would *have* in it or in terms of the bundle swaps they would be willing to make? How this is answered bears on the question of which allocations pass the test. Let the bundles be close in size, however their sizes are measured. Envy then is less common on the bundle-swaps reading, for there may be some status-quo bias. So on

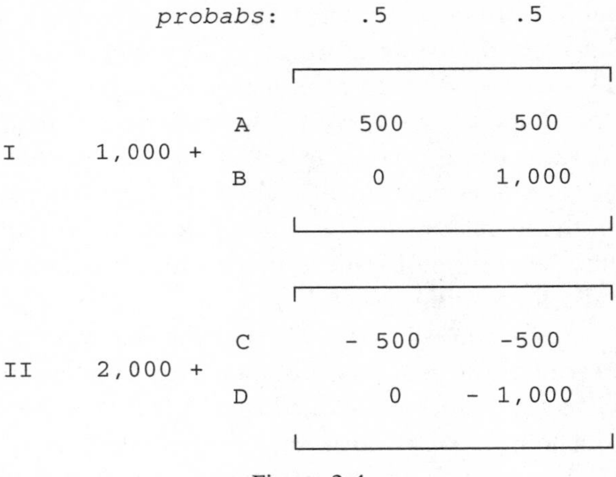

Figure 3.4

that reading more allocations pass.[32] But is that the reading to take?[33]

4

We have been speaking of gains and losses in a context of certainty. What about cases in which we are choosing and acting under risk?

Here is a well-known Kahneman and Tversky experiment. Each of a group of people was put into one of two situations. Those in Situation I were told to imagine they had received 1,000 (say, in dollars) and were asked to choose between A: getting another 500 for sure and B: an even chance of nothing more or getting another 1,000. Those in Situation II were told to imagine they were given *2,000* and asked to choose between C: *losing* 500 and D: an even chance of nothing further or losing 1,000. The two situations are shown in Figure 3.4. The vast majority of the people in I chose A. The vast majority in II chose D. The placings in situations having been random, we can infer that most of the people in these two sets inclined both to A and to D (or would have, if they had both as options).

Kahneman and Tversky say that this result is "clearly inconsistent with utility theory,"[34] this because the foreseeable outcomes of A and of C were objectively the same (a total of 1,500), and also those of B and of D (an even chance of 1,000 or 2,000). In their view, utility theory takes the "carriers of value" to be objective conditions, however these are described. Still, the result is not inconsistent with a *subjective* utility theory in which the foci of valuation (the "carriers of value") are propositions – conditions under *these* or *those* descriptions.[35]

What accounts for the A-and-D choosers (plus all the *would-have-been* A-and-D'ers)? I suggest that they saw the outcomes in terms of their foreseen gains and losses. These they measured from the sums just received, which were different in the two situations (in I, they were given 1,000; in II, they were given 2,000). The foreseen gains and losses were thus different too. Option A offered a gain of 500, and option C offered a loss of 500.[36] The choosers (I assume) were loss averse, and the *S*-curve of loss aversion implies risk aversion for gains and risk inclination for losses. This means that these people valued the outcome of B (a gamble on gains) at *less* than a gain of 500 and that of D (a gamble on losses) at *more* than a loss of 500. So they opted for A over B and for D over C.

How can we account for the A-and-C choosers? I suggest that they saw the outcomes as it seems Kahneman and Tversky did, in terms of all they would have in them: as then having x dollars, not as having x' more (or x' less) than they had at the start. So seen, the outcomes of A are the same as those of C, and those of B are the same as those of D. Each of the outcomes, so seen, being positive, only risk aversion entered; risk inclination didn't. These people too ranked A above B (in their *havings* view of them), but they ranked C above D, and so they opted for A and for C. On this analysis of how they all chose, both the A-and-C'ers and the A-and-D'ers were being rational. The difference between them was that they saw the possible outcomes differently, which wired-up different values for them.

A question like one we touched on before: how *should* they have seen the outcomes? It is a basic tenet of economics that "fixed, historical and other sunk costs do not [*should* not] influence decisions,"[37] and so too for fixed (deposited) gains; that "only incremental costs and benefits should affect decisions."[38] The up-front sums in I and II being fixed, a good economist would have ignored them – the A-and-D'ers saw things correctly and the A-and-C'ers didn't. The A-and-C'ers can, however, cite another tenet of economics, that of asset integration; that "the domain of the utility function is final states,"[39] that only the total assets we expect to have in them may count for us. On this, it was the A-and-C'ers who were seeing things right. But in fact neither tenet is law; there can't be a law about how one *should* think. The question of *shoulds* remains.

The up-front sums having come in the past isn't the central factor here. What is central is that the A-and-D'ers excluded these sums from their view of the outcomes. Let me change things slightly. Suppose that the people in I were told that they must choose either A or B and that they *then* would be given 1,000 – and another 500 if they chose A, etc. Suppose that those in II were told that they must choose either C or D and *then* would get 2,000 – minus 500 if they chose C, etc. Here there would be no fixed gains in the past, but rather the promise of sure-thing gains, of *exogenous* gains (the 1,000 or 2,000 dollars), gains independent of whatever was chosen. The choices are nonetheless likely to resemble those in the Figure 3.4 case. The people who there were A-and-D'ers are likely to also be A-and-D'ers here; since fixed, past gains didn't enter their thinking, neither will exogenous *future* gains. And correspondingly for the A-and-C'ers.

Here too we can speak of the A-and-D'ers as going by changes from their basing points, but note that in this modified

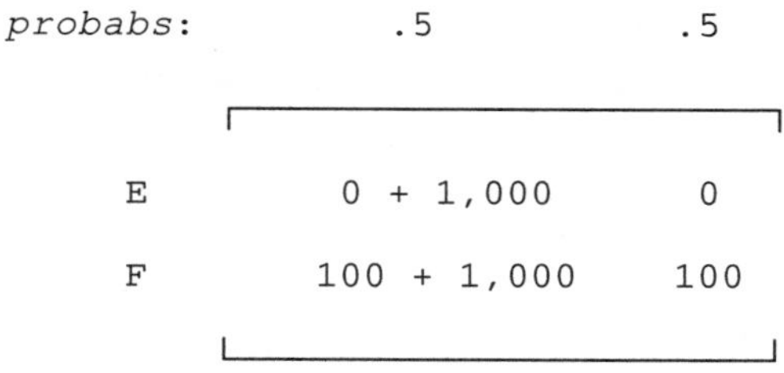

probabs:	.5	.5
E	0 + 1,000	0
F	100 + 1,000	100

Figure 3.5

case the basing points aren't what the agent now *has*. His future sure-things aren't yet had, though he can count on his getting them. This suggests a further extension. Say you can't count on that 1,000 or 2,000 – you can't be sure you will get it. But you are sure you *would* get it if a certain contingency held: you know it to be a *contingent* gain, a contingent *exogenous* gain. (It is *exogenous* for you in that you would get it however you chose.) If you now think in terms of the changes you might bring about by your choosing, a contingent exogenous gain serves as a basing point (or a part of one) for you – call it a *contingent* basing point.

Suppose that, in Situation I, the experimenter doesn't offer to give you 1,000 after you have chosen but offers then to toss a coin and to give you 1,000 only if it falls heads. Or take this different case. Again, you have two options. If you choose E, you will (at first) get nothing; if you choose F, you will (at first) get 100. The experimenter will then toss a coin and give you 1,000 if it falls heads. That possible extra 1,000 is a heads-contingent exogenous gain, and that 1,000 (plus whatever you have) is your heads-contingent basing point. Your *tails*-contingent basing point is zero (plus . . .). This case appears in Figure 3.5.

You are bound to choose F here however you see the outcomes. If you are looking to what you would gain over your contingent basing points, you will ignore the 1,000 in Column 1, that being (part of) what in Column 1 you are counting your gains *from*. F is then better than E for you. If you are looking to what you would gain over what you already have, you will count that 1,000, and F remains better than E. And so too if you go by your *havings*, if you integrate assets; F remains better than E.

But consider one last twist. Again, if you choose E, you will (at first) get nothing, and if you choose F, you will (at first) get 100. This time, however, the experimenter won't toss a coin. He will give you the extra 1,000 if he predicted beforehand that you would take E. (He will give you that 1,000 whatever it turns out you did.) If he predicted you would take F, he will give you nothing. You know he predicted one or the other and that he is such a clever predictor that, whatever you now choose, there is a .99 probability he predicted you will do it. Figure 3.5 reports this too if we put in different (here *conditional*) probabilities. In the first column, the experimenter predicted you will take E – let that be PE; in the second, he predicted you will take F – this is PF. So the probabilities both of PE given E and of PF given F are .99, and both *p*(PE,F) and *p*(PF,E) are .01.

This is the familiar Newcomb case.[40] Some people here choose F, other people choose E. Is F still better than E? Are the E-choosers wrong? Say that the F-choosers look to their gains and that they do that selectively, screening out the exogenous ones. Since how they now choose can't affect how the predictor predicted, their getting the PE-contingent 1,000 isn't now up to them and they leave it out of account; only the *endogenous*, up-to-them gains of 100 enter their thinking. So the expected utility of F is greater for them than that of E, and they are right to choose F. Say that the E-choosers too are looking to what they might gain but view their gains *inclusively*, those that would be exogenous included. (Or they look to their final havings, which here comes to the same.) If so, the expected utility of E exceeds that of F, and they rightly choose E. Again, how the outcomes are seen can matter.[41]

Going by gains from contingent basing points often calls for more discernment than does going by gains from sure-things. The problem is spotting exogeny. In the Newcomb case, the exogeny of the PE-contingent 1,000 is clear. In other cases, exogeny may be masked by how the cases are put. Look again at Figure 3.4. Perhaps the A-and-D'ers didn't notice that the entries in Column 2 included, in Situation I, a (contingent) exogenous gain of 500 and, in Situation II, a (contingent) exogenous loss of 500. Had they noticed it, they might have rethought. They might have subtracted these gains and losses from the entries in that column, which would have left each matrix symmetrical with regard to its options. These people would then have been indifferent both between A and B and between C and D and might then have chosen A and C. (This reopens the question of why the A-and-C'ers chose as they did. Perhaps they went by their havings, by their foreseen assets *in toto,* as I suggested above. Perhaps, however, some of them went by their foreseen gains and losses, but only by those that weren't exogenous to their choices and actions.)

5

In this section, a puzzle and a solution, though a solution that raises new questions.

Suppose we replotted the points on the gain/loss curves in Figure 3.3, this time letting x be on the vertical axis and y on the horizontal. That would give us Figure 3.6. Does this figure present the agent's gain/loss curves with regard to y? The new curves exhibit loss aversion (and the endowment effect and status-quo bias). But here it may seem that the sensitivity to gains and losses increases with their size, that increasingly larger gains/losses are assigned *increasingly* greater value/disvalue. In Figure 3.3, the sensitivity to changes *decreases;* and for gains and losses of a normal good (and a

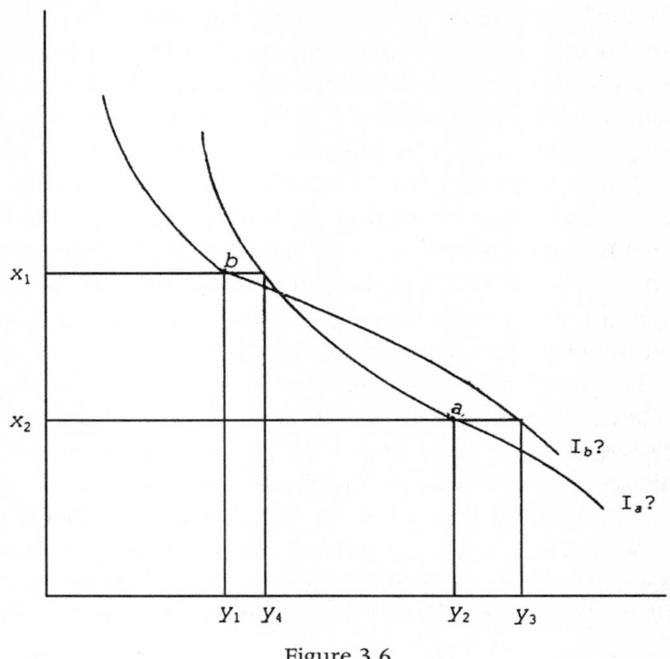

Figure 3.6

normal agent), Figure 3.3 gets it right. How can Figure 3.6 show the contrary?

The figures are wholly congruent – each is a spatial transformation of the other. (Rotate Figure 3.3 clockwise 90 degrees, and then turn the resulting graph 180 degrees around its horizontal axis; that gives you Figure 3.6.) They are, in that sense, the same, but the agent reads them differently, and the puzzle derives from ignoring the difference in his readings of them. It stems from ignoring the fact that he sees changes in x and y differently, seeing changes in x as gains or losses and changes in y as neither.

How can a change be seen as neither a gain nor a loss? Both a person's gains and the compensations he gets for his losses are increments of this or that asset. Both his losses and his payments (outlays, expenses) are decrements of his assets. But his different assets differ in priority for him. He sees an increment as a *gain* if it augments what he has of some asset of main concern to him, an asset he now is trying to augment or preserve. He sees it as a *compensation* if it augments what he has of some secondary asset. Correspondingly for losses and payments: he calls a decrement a *loss* if it diminishes what he has of some now-primary asset, he calls it a *payment* if it diminishes what he has of some now-secondary asset. (Compensations and payments always are parts of some larger picture, a compensation being *for some loss*, a payment being *for some gain*. Gains and losses stand on their own.)

The agent in all the above is mainly concerned with *x*, not with *y*. What he sees as his gains and losses – his changes in *x* – are laid out in Figure 3.3 horizontally. The curves in 3.3 are his g/l curves and they exhibit diminishing sensitivity to *x*, to his gains and losses. The curves in Figure 3.6 exhibit increasing sensitivity to changes in *y*, but since these aren't seen by the agent as being gains and losses for him, this doesn't show that his sensitivity to gains and losses increases here. What it shows is that his sensitivity *to compensations and payments* increases.[42] The curves in 3.3 are g/l curves and those in 3.6 are c/p curves, and the curves accord with each other.

When is an asset primary; when is it "of main concern"? When is it only secondary?[43] The answers have to do with the agent's intentions, with what he is trying to preserve or augment, or would have tried to preserve or augment if he had the chance. (He would have tried to keep his house from burning down if he could have. The house was of main concern to him; thus he now sees the insurance money as compensation, not as a gain.) Still, the concepts of *intentions* and *trying* are themselves unclear, so a different (or a fuller) answer to our last questions would be welcome.

4

IN SUPPORT OF PERSUASION

THE common theory of motivation refers to what people want and believe. It speaks of motives as *reasons*, and it holds that people's reasons are composed of desires and beliefs, that a person has a reason for choosing (and for doing) *a* where he wants to choose (or take) an action of a certain sort *b* and believes *a* is of sort *b*. I have argued that this is too thin, that we need to bring in also how he sees or understands *a*, that he has a reason for choosing (and for doing) *a* where he wants to choose (or take) an action of a certain sort *b* and believes *a* is of sort *b* – and *sees a* as being of that sort.[1] This seems to me not only correct but useful and suggestive. Others resist the idea. What are their grounds for resisting it?

1

My three-part idea brings in people's seeings. These are not seeings of houses or trees but of *actions* or *events* or *situations* – I will use "situations" as a catchall for this. They are our *grasps* of those situations, our *construals* or *understandings* of them. They are our reports of them (to ourselves), our *conceivings* of them. Such *seeings-as* aren't retinal; the blind have no problem with them. An inner eye is engaged.

This last only adds a metaphor to a long string of synonyms. The question remains: what *are* such seeings? And to that question I have no answer. I think the concept can't be defined in any noncircular way, that it is too basic a concept to be laid out in terms of others. Beliefs and desires are equally basic and equally undefinable. But we don't always need definitions. We can make do with instances, letting these show how our concepts apply, or how they function, along with some others, in a general theory. Negative remarks may be helpful here too, remarks on what seeings are *not*.

The basic negative point is this, that seeings aren't believings. Our seeing of some situation as *p* isn't the same as our believing *p*.[2] There is indeed a connection, for the seeing implies the belief: we can see a situation as *p* only if we now believe *p*. Still, the converse doesn't hold. Our seeing of a situation always is selective. It selects from the propositions we believe report that situation.[3] And it selects uniquely; this or that can be differently seen, but we can't at any moment see it in more than one way – though that way may be conjunctive, the conjuncts then being only *partial* seeings. Say we believe that Smith won the election. We can see his having won as *Smith won the election*. Or we can see it as *Jones lost* or as *Smith won and Jones lost*. But we can't see it in one of these ways and also in one of the others.

A second negative point: seeings, unlike beliefs and desires, aren't propositional attitudes. You see situations as *p* or as *q*, as some propositions or other, but *what* you then see – the *objects* of your seeings – are not propositions. Rather, they are the situations that these or those propositions report. True, the object of your seeing-*that p* (that *Smith won*) is a proposition. But seeings-*that* aren't seeings-*as*, though wherever you see *that p* you also see some situation *as p*. Again, we are speaking of seeings-as here, and these are *situational* attitudes.[4]

These negative points don't take us far. In the end, we have to resort to calling up clear cases of seeings, or to calling up distinctions that are based on the concept. One such distinction has to do with how we change people's minds. Say that we want to get a person to do what he doesn't now want to do. He doesn't believe it will serve any purpose. If we can get him to reconsider, we may get him to act, so we try to convince him. To *convince* a person is to change his beliefs, to get him to believe what he didn't before.

Sometimes the change we hope to arrange is not in the other's beliefs. He lacks some desire we want him to have and we try to instill that desire. We try to get him to want what he doesn't – we try to *induce* him to want it. And sometimes too we take a third course. We try to get him to see the action in a way he didn't before – as an obligation he has, or as an act of kindness, or as a test of friendship. In such cases, we speak of *persuasion*, a changing not of beliefs or desires but of the other's *seeing* of things. Here that seeing is of some action we want him now to take, but it may be of events in the past, or of the prospects of some action, or of anything else. A persuasion is a deliberate changing of someone's seeing of something.[5]

We need a good instance of this. Think of Melville's *Billy Budd*, at the center of which is a sudden shipboard death. Billy, a simple sailor, had been accused of inciting to mutiny. The charge was a lie, and Billy had struck his accuser and killed him. All on board knew he was innocent of the charge, and they all knew he hadn't meant to kill. But a man had in fact been killed, and the Captain appointed a jury of officers for a trial.

The officers inclined to be lenient. Clearly, there was no evil intent; the blow had been an act of passion, a reaction to being slandered. None of them wanted to hang a person who had committed no moral crime. The Captain addressed their scruples:

> [Does the] deed constitute a capital crime whereof the penalty is a mortal one? . . . [I]s nothing but the prisoner's overt act to be considered? . . . [C]an we adjudge to a summary and shameful death a fellow-creature innocent before God, and whom we feel to be so? – Does that state it right? . . . Well, I too feel . . . the full force of [these scruples]. It is Nature. But do

> these buttons that we wear attest that our allegiance is to Nature? No, to the King. . . . [A]s the King's officers, lies our duty in a sphere [that is] natural? [No, for] . . . in receiving our commissions, we in the most important regards ceased to be natural free-agents. When war is declared, . . . [w]e fight at command. If our judgments approve the war, that is but coincidence. So in other particulars. So now."[6]

He went on to remind the officers that they were in fact at war, that they were governed by the Articles of War, that the man whom Billy had killed was his superior in rank, which alone made it mutiny – all of which they knew. He then left them to think it through, and they reluctantly sentenced Billy to be hanged.

The Captain had brought them over, but he hadn't changed the beliefs they had been ready to act on. (He may have changed their beliefs *about him*, but those were no part of why they voted as they did.) What they had wanted was unchanged too. They had wanted not to hang someone who was morally innocent, and they still wanted not to do this – hence their reluctance to the very end. And they had wanted all along to act as dutiful officers of the King. The Captain had convinced them of nothing and he induced no change in their values, but he did persuade them. He got them no longer to see Billy's action as "innocent before God." He got them to see it instead as violating the Articles of War.

The officers knew Billy to be morally innocent. They wanted to avoid the injustice of hanging a morally innocent man and they knew that a lenient sentence would avoid that injustice. They would have voted for lenience had they continued to see being lenient as the sparing of an innocent. But the persuasion had got them to see Billy's action as mutinous and to see both lenience and harshness in terms of responding to mutiny. Their minds then being turned to that, they voted to have him hanged.

2

I want to consider some common objections to speaking of seeings in a theory of reasons. It will help to bring them to bear on what happens in *Billy Budd*.

The first objection is that my theory takes in more than it needs. I said that the Captain didn't convince the officers to change the beliefs that they had. Also, that he didn't get them to change what they wanted or (more broadly) their values, that instead he persuaded them to change how they saw their options. The critic says that he did change their values, that he got them to want Billy hanged. Persuasions work on how things are seen, but they only work on seeings in order to change what people want. A persuasion is a seduction; it gets its way indirectly. Its purpose is to rouse a desire, and that desire plus some belief often then compose a reason. A proper theory of reasons lets them be just two-part affairs, one part a desire, the other a belief. How things are seen doesn't enter.

True, the Captain's persuasion got the officers to want Billy hanged. But their wanting that wasn't part of the reason the Captain gave them. Their wanting that (or their coming to want it) was what he gave them a reason *for*. Wanting Billy hanged wasn't part of what moved them but what they moved *to*.

Besides, how did their being persuaded get them to come to want Billy hanged – how did it *rouse* their wanting that? On the critic's two-part theory, we have a reason for choosing some *a* (that is, for coming to want it) where we want to choose an action of a certain sort *b* and believe *a* is of sort *b*. This says nothing about persuasion, about how that plays a role. On my theory, we have a reason for choosing (for coming to want) some *a* where we want to choose an action of sort *b* and believe *a* is of that sort *and see a as being of that sort*. Persuasions change people's seeings. Thus they get them to come to want *a* (to *choose* it) where their new seeing is part of their reason for coming to want *a* (for choosing *a*).[7]

The critic might change the line he is taking. I have said that the officers wanted *not* to hang an innocent man. They also wanted to punish mutiny; they wanted both all along. The Captain got them to see the issue in terms of responding to mutiny, which wired-up the latter desire and put them in favor of Billy's being hanged. The other desire remained, but now unwired, inoperative. The critic might say this instead, that when they saw the issue in terms of responding to a mutiny, the officers *ceased to want* (right there!) not to hang an innocent man; that the persuasion succeeded by *subduing* a certain desire they had, their ceasing to want not to hang someone innocent undoing their reason not to hang such a person. New seeings may sometimes discredit certain reasons, but reasons themselves don't include any seeings.

Did the officers cease to want not to hang an innocent man? Melville clearly wants us to think that their vote was reluctant, that they wanted to punish mutiny but continued *not* to want to hang a person who was innocent. In real life too, reluctance is common, people reporting their being unhappy about some choice they are making. I suggest this says that these people are in an inner conflict, that the choice, say of *a*, they are making is based on desire *d* that they have where they also have some desire *d′* they think incompatible with it.[8] Let us speak only of cases (like the officers') in which they believe they might gratify either; they don't think *d′* out of reach. They base their choice on their siding with *d* and against *d′* – on their seeing *a* in a way that wires-up desire *d* and not seeing any *a′* in a way that wires-up *d′* (though they *know* of some option they have that would satisfy *d′*).[9] On this analysis, *d′* remains even where they wire-up *d*, which keeps their choice of *a* halfhearted.

In Melville's story, *a* is hanging Billy, *d* is wanting to uphold the law, and *d′* is wanting to spare an innocent. The officers knew that *a* would satisfy *d*. They knew that their other option *a′*, lenience, would satisfy *d′*. The Captain's persuasion had got them to side with *d* and against *d'*; it had got them to see both hanging and being lenient in terms of the law. So they chose *a*, but since *d'* remained, the choice they then made was reluctant. The critic rejects this reading – he denies that *d'* remained – but what does he put in its place? How does he interpret reluctance?

Think too of weakness of will. A person wants both *p* and *p'* (these are propositions), wanting *p'* more.[10] He believes action *a* would yield *p* (that it would make *p* true) and that *a'* would yield *p'*. He thinks he could take either *a* or *a'* but that he can't take both. If he chooses (or takes) action *a*, he makes that choice reluctantly, this because he still wants *p'*. We speak of weakness of will in this case because he not only still wants *p'* but wants it more than what his choice will yield.

Weakness of will is often considered a psychological puzzle. On my theory, it isn't puzzling, at least in most cases it isn't. On my theory, it has to do with lacking a full reason for choosing *a'*, the facially better option. Say that the person just above sees *a* as yielding (making true) *p*. Say that he doesn't see *a'* as yielding *p'*, though he *thinks* that it would – he sees *a'* in some other way. Given the beliefs and desires he has, he then has a full (three-part) reason for *a* but lacks a full reason for *a'*. He isn't moved to take *a'*, though he thinks it would yield *p'*, which he wants more than *p*.

A man loves a woman and wants to live with her (*p'*). He also wants not to abandon his wife (*p*), though he wants that less. He may in the end choose not to leave, this with a heavy heart, for it may be that he can't see his leaving as his joining the other woman but only as an abandonment. Or, again, the officers: they wanted to spare an innocent man and also to uphold the law. Say that they wanted the former more but voted against a lenient sentence because they saw their voting for that not as sparing an innocent but as encouraging crime. If so, then, like the stay-at-home husband, they revealed weakness of will. (Though weakness of will, on my analysis, isn't a failing and needn't be faulted.)

The critic's two-part theory of reasons doesn't allow for seeings. What then can he say about this? He can say that there never is weakness, that the husband's staying at home shows that he wanted that most, that the way the officers voted showed what *they* wanted most, etc. He can say that no choice is reluctant, that there never is inner conflict at a point of choice, that a chooser never sides with one desire against some other. This would go against what people often claim to experience, but the critic could shrug that off: if there isn't any reluctance or weakness of will and the like, people who say they experience these matters can be considered confused.

Or he may admit reluctance and admit weakness too, but then add that, where they enter, the reasons we have don't explain how we choose. (They don't explain why someone chooses a and not a' instead.) On my theory, they do explain it, which counts in support of that theory.

3

The first objection was that reasons never involve any seeings. The next two objections only hold that *sometimes* reasons don't involve seeings, that, in certain common cases, how things are seen can make no difference. These are the cases in which people's thinking keeps to a suitable logic. The claim is that the constraints of that logic leave people's seeings with nothing to do, or nothing that wouldn't be done by beliefs in a belief/desire theory.

Here is one such constraint of logic, a principle applying to beliefs and values jointly – call it the principle of *extensionality*. Suppose you believe that p and q report the same situation;[11] the principle requires you to set on q whatever value you set on p. If you want one, you must want the other. If you prefer one of the two to a third, you must prefer the other to it. You must set the same utility on them. Say you adhere to this principle. How you *see* the situation reported – whether you see it as *p* or as *q* – can't then make any difference, for, whichever way you see it, you wire-up the same values. The values that you choose (and act) upon are the same however you see things.[12]

Once more, to *Billy Budd*. The officers knew that hanging Billy would be upholding the law. They also knew that hanging him would be hanging an innocent man. They knew that *p*: *We hang someone innocent* and *q*: *We uphold the law* were coreportive. Had they adhered to extensionality, they would have valued *p* and *q* the same. (They would not have wanted *q* and ~*p*, as they did in the story.) Whatever they then chose to do, they could have chosen without hesitation, for their choice would not have discorded with anything they wanted to do. There could have been no reluctance involved, for they would have been in no conflict. And no change in how they saw things could have made any difference to them. So too beyond the officers' case: where there is extensionality, there can't be conflict and can't be reluctance. There can be no weakness of will. And a persuasion is not worth the effort – not even where the persuasion succeeds, where it changes how things are seen.

I have argued that the principle of extensionality should be rejected.[13] Most writers today disagree. Daniel Kahneman and Amos Tversky refer to the principle as that of *invariance*, and they hold that "invariance is normatively essential [and] intuitively compelling."[14] Isaac Levi speaks of *robustness* (imperviousness to persuasion), and he too thinks that is a virtue.[15] The point seems to be that value-setting must be constrained by what we believe. Yes, but how tightly constrained? Where we believe *p* and *q* coreportive – and so believe either both or neither – must we set the same value on them? The principle of extensionality says that we must, but no argument ever is offered in support of that principle. The principle is simply assumed.[16]

Those who accept extensionality make no case for accepting it. What case do I have for rejecting it? I have a general policy that applies to all principles. The basic idea is that of a sort of balancing or equilibrium – an equilibrium in *thought*, a *reflective* equilibrium. As Nelson Goodman puts it, our principles and judgments "are justified by being brought into agreement with each other. A [principle] is amended [or rejected] if it yields a [judgment] we are unwilling to accept; a [judgment] is rejected if it violates a [principle] we are unwilling to amend."[17]

How does this work for me here? If I accepted extensionality, I would have to say (to "judge") that the officers' inner conflicts were foolish. I would have to say the same about the agonized husband. He wanted not to leave home; had he adhered to logic, he would have wanted to end his affair and would have lost nothing he wanted. I would have to fault weakness of will and indeed all reluctance. I would have to consider persuasion always a waste of time (except where directed at illogical people). These are judgments I don't want to make. To my mind (as also to Melville's), the officers' reluctance was a credit to them. The husband's anguish calls for respect, not for a lecture in logic. Extensionality directs me to judgments I refuse to accept, so the policy of reaching for equilibrium obliges me to reject it. (Must the reader reject it too? That depends on *his* view of these judgments.)[18]

4

The extensionality idea applies to our beliefs and our values jointly. The second constraint applies to our beliefs and *seeings*. It holds that we must see every situation as the conjunction of all we believe about it. Say you believe that *p*, *q*, and *r* are about situation *s* (perhaps an action *a*), that you believe these three propositions and believe of no other proposition (logically independent of them) that it too is about *s*.[19] You must then *see* that situation as *p*-and-*q*-and-*r*. Call this the *total-belief* principle.[20]

Those who adhere to this principle can still be said to have three-part reasons. Their seeings can still be allowed a role, but that role then only echoes the role their beliefs are playing. What they believe determines their seeings, which thus become mere hangers-on. A theory of reasons for these people could avoid all mention of seeings. It could say that these people have a reason for choosing some *a* where they believe *a* is of sort *b* and (perhaps) also of sort *b′* and (perhaps) also of sort *b″* – this exhausting their beliefs about *a* – and they want to choose an action of sort *b*-and-*b′*-and-*b″*. There would be no need to add that they *see a* as *b*-and-*b′*-and-*b″*. That would follow from their adhering to the total-belief principle.

Another way of putting it: where we weigh our options, all that we know about them counts. Nothing we know may be set aside, and our seeings must reflect this. They can't just select from what we know or believe. This connects with the common idea that a reasonable person always acts on his evidence, *all considered*. To act on our evidence, all considered, is to leave nothing out of the picture, to let no mere part of what we believe determine the choice that we make. Donald Davidson presents this idea as a principle of *continence*, using that term because the principle disallows weakness of will (which he labels in the usual, narrow way as *in*continence).[21]

How would this principle apply in our cases? In general, the more inclusive the seeings, the less they serve to motivate. The officers chose on the basis of seeing the hanging as upholding the law. They knew that Billy was blameless, but they put that out of their minds. Had they adhered to the principle, they would have seen their hanging Billy as upholding the law *and* hanging the blameless; and since they didn't want to choose to take some action of this compound sort (didn't want to be law-upholding *and* blameless-person-hanging), they would have had no reason to do it. Given what they believed and wanted, they would have had no reason for being lenient with him either – they didn't want to acquit the blameless *and* to ignore the law. Their seeings wouldn't have connected what they believed with anything that they wanted. If the husband in our other story had adhered to the principle, he would have had no reason either for staying or for leaving – he wanted neither to join his love *and* to abandon his wife nor to remain with his wife *and* to give up love. (He would not, as above, have had a weak-willed reason for staying.)

Here is still another case. A judge has been offered a bribe. He says, "That's a bribe, and I don't take bribes." His friend says, "It is a lot of money; it would be a *benefaction*. It is also a rare opportunity. OK, yes, it is a bribe, but see it as a bribe-*and*-benefaction-*and*-opportunity. Keep in mind all you know about it – always see the whole picture!" The judge replies, "I see a bribe as a bribe."

May we side with the judge? May we reject the total-belief rule? Again, reflective equilibrium: we have to reject if it yields judgments that we refuse to accept. The rule would fault the judge for closing his mind to the tempter. It would fault the officers and the husband for seeing things as they did. I can't (or won't) accept these judgments. I can't accept this blanket censure of being selective in how things are seen, so I reject the rule.[22]

We have noted that in some contexts the rule would tie our hands fully. To get to that from a different direction (from the logic of prediction), think of Goodman's blue/bleen problem.[23] Each of the many marbles drawn from an urn was blue. Each was also *bleen*, a bleen marble being one that is either drawn before midnight tonight and is blue or drawn after and is green. We report the draws, we *see* them, as being of blues, not of bleens. That lets us predict that the first marble drawn after midnight will be blue and keeps us from predicting also (or instead) that it will be bleen. This is the core of Goodman's theory of why we here predict *this* and not *that*[24] – better, it is my gloss on his theory.

If we adhered to the total-belief rule, we would see the draws as being of marbles that were blue *and also* bleen, which would not only keep us from predicting that some post-midnight marble will be bleen but keep us from predicting that it will be blue. (Each prediction would be blocked by the other, and each would have equal force.) Predicting its being both blue and bleen would be ruled out too, for that would imply (by definition) that it will be both blue and *green*, which we dismiss a priori. Since a Goodmanian doppelgänger exists for every descriptive term (as with blue/bleen, so with light/leavy, soft/sard, etc.), *every* prediction would be ruled out, both here and everywhere else. Too much to pay for a rule of thought!

Often the rule is modified slightly. It then directs you to see action *a* as the conjunction of your *relevant* beliefs about it (of what you believe in them). Which of your beliefs count as relevant for you in a choice-and-action context? Here is a possible answer.[25] Believing-*r* is relevant for you where believing *p*-and-*q*-and-*r* . . . gives you a two-part, belief/desire reason either for *a* or against it and believing *p*-and-*q* . . . (*r* left out) . . . does not.

This still leaves the rule too strong. The judge's believing that taking the money would make him rich (plus his wanting to be rich) gives him a (belief/desire) reason for taking it, a reason he wouldn't otherwise have; so this belief is relevant for him in the proposed sense of relevance. His belief that taking the money would be taking a bribe gives him a reason *against* taking it he wouldn't have if he didn't believe *that*, so this belief too is relevant. The modified rule thus sides with the tempter: the judge ought to see his taking the money as taking a bribe *and* making himself rich. I have been saying he may well see it as just taking a bribe, which argues against the rule. (But doesn't endorsing such selectivity stack the cards against it? Yes, but no more so than endorsing the rule would stack the cards against selectivity.)

Perhaps some other concept of relevance might be considered instead. We might perhaps take believing-*r* to be relevant where we *see a* as *r*. But, in this context, that wouldn't do, for the rule of total-relevant-belief couldn't then govern our seeings of things.

5

Note that the Captain's persuasion worked. It got the others to change how they saw what Billy did and his being hanged for it. It did this by telling them how they *ought* to see that, by stressing the wrongness of their initial view of it. This raises a question that is seldom asked: when is a person seeing things *rightly*? What makes some seeings *right* and some *wrong*?

The neglect of this question reflects the usual neglect of seeings themselves.[26] But even writers who don't neglect seeings avoid this difficult question. Aristotle does it by definition. His word for seeings translates as "understandings," and he holds that these *must* be right, for "[u]nderstanding is identical with goodness of understanding, men of understanding with men of good understanding."[27] That makes his concept different from mine, which doesn't have rightness built into it. It disallows the question here of *when* we are seeing things rightly. (Still, *this* question might have been asked: when does a person understand things and when does he only think he does, and Aristotle doesn't ask it.)

So too for Kant, whose word for seeing is translated as "judgment." Kant speaks of judgment as the application of rules (or laws or principles or the like), as the "subsuming" of situations, as the grasping or seeing of them so that this or that rule applies. He then quickly folds that concept into that of *right* judgment. He holds that the power of *rightly* applying rules is a "natural gift" – either you have it or you don't. It is "a peculiar talent which can be practiced only, and cannot be taught."[28] An exercise of this special talent yields a right judgment by definition. Our question becomes what is and what isn't an exercise of this talent. When is a person judging rightly? Again, when is he seeing things right?

It may be suggested that seeings are right where they follow nature, where they focus on natural kinds, on the shared properties of classes of things to which the same laws of nature apply. That would leave us the messy issue of which classes (which "kinds") are natural. (What counts as a law *of nature*?) And it wouldn't take us far, however that issue is settled. Seeing your eating these berries as eating *blue*berries may be right and as eating *bleen*berries wrong, and perhaps blueberries form a natural class and bleenberries don't.[29] But what about that bribe to the judge? The judge insisted on seeing it as a bribe; he held that that was the *right* way to see it, that seeing it as a benefaction was wrong. Do bribes form a natural class and benefactions not? Also, which form a more natural class, abandonments of long-standing spouses or turnings to people one loves, hangings of people to uphold the law or hangings of the innocent?

We come back to the Captain's persuasion. To what did it make its appeal? The officers saw the hanging of Billy as the hanging of an innocent. The Captain had to persuade them to see it as upholding the law. He reminded them that they were officers and that an officer took the King's view. Where some action affected the King, an officer had to attend to that, whatever else he might think of it. He had to see a mutiny as just being a mutiny. He had to see Billy's hanging for it as what the law demanded. The Captain was speaking of what was central to a naval man's way of life. This way of life was one he knew his officers all endorsed, a way of life to which he knew they wanted to conform their own. He got them to change their view of the case by turning their minds to their larger project, the project of being good officers, and by showing them what that implied, what it committed them to.

The Captain's appeal was to inner cohesion: if you want to be a person who sees certain things *like this*, you must want to see them so, and if you want to see them so, that is how you should see them.[30] He reminded his officers of what they wanted to be, and he argued that what they wanted called for their seeing the case as he put it. In his own mind, and in theirs too, that seeing was *right* – it was right *for them* – because their leading the life they had chosen called for that view of the case.

Here is a different persuasion, this one in Jane Austen's *Persuasion*. Some time before that novel opens, Anne had loved and wanted to marry a man who loved and wanted her. In himself, he was perfect for her, but Lady Russell, an older friend, didn't think he would do. Lady Russell "...had prejudices on the side of ancestry, ... a value for rank and consequence.... [For] Anne Elliot [to] involve herself at nineteen in an engagement with a young man who had nothing but himself to recommend him, and no hopes of attaining affluence ... and no connections ... would be indeed a throwing away, which she grieved to think of!"[31] She saw it as an unsuitable match and got Anne to see it so too.

How did she persuade her? Austen suggests that Anne had mixed feelings. Brought up as a baronet's daughter, she too inclined, if halfheartedly only, to a life of "rank and consequence," a life of "affluence ... and connections." Having been focused by Lady Russell on her desire to lead such a life, she came to reflect on what leading it meant in the situation she found herself in. That then got her to concede that the match was unsuitable.

Here we have a desire d to lead a certain sort of life and a way of seeing things that is a part of leading it. Desire d calls for d', for wanting to see things that way. This in turn calls for seeing it so – which is thus called for by d. Anne's rank-and-consequence desire d called for her seeing the match as she did, and since she knew that (and acknowledged d), she came to think that view of it *right*. Its being right in this narrow sense, we can say it was right *for her*.

Again we locate the rightness of seeings in their cohesion with certain desires, with the agent's wanting to be the kind of person who sees things *like that.*[32] We find their rightness in their fitting with certain other mental states. The critic reenters here. He thinks that a weird sort of rightness; since we are free to want what we please, it lets us (he holds) suit our whims and our fancies. It leaves how we see things up to us. It tells us that anything goes.

The critic ignores the limitations the logic of wanting imposes. As with belief, so with desire – every desire lies under constraints. Say we want people (or people like us) to live in a certain way; we must then want to live that way too. Wanting *p*, we must want *q*, if we think *q* is requisite for it, and we must want $\sim r$ if we think *r* would block or defeat it. These *musts* extend in every direction and compose a fabric of wantings that is under still further constraints.

This last deserves a closer look. W. V. Quine says about beliefs:

> The totality of our . . . beliefs . . . is a man-made fabric which impinges on experience only along the edges. . . . A conflict with experience at the periphery occasions readjustments in the interior of the field. . . . Reëvaluations of some statements entails reëvaluation of others because of their logical interconnections. . . . But the total field is so underdetermined by its boundary conditions, experience, that there is much latitude of choice as to what statements to reëvaluate in the light of any single contrary experience.[33]

Beliefs are constrained by experience, an exogenous ("peripheral") constraint, though there remains "much latitude." If we put "needs" in place of "experience," this carries over to wantings: wantings are constrained by *needs*. (That is, if needs are other than wantings. A fabric, whether of beliefs or desires, can "impinge" only on what is outside it.)

This takes us beyond *Billy Budd*, where the talk is solely of duties; needs don't there enter the picture. In Austen's *Persuasion*, they do. Anne wanted to follow the rules of her class and also to be guided by Lady Russell, who pointed her in the same direction. She also wanted the best for Frederick and believed she was doing that. Her wantings formed a coherent whole. Still, her acting on her desire to keep to her class was a self-denial, for she soon found that she yearned for Frederick, that she needed to have him. Her values had failed the test of her needs, and the novel is the story of her "reëvaluations," of how she came to have new values that she then could live with.

This speaks of desires only. But our acting on a desire brings in other matters too. Say that we have some desire *d*. To act on *d* is to take some action that we *believe* will satisfy *d* where we *see* that action as one that will satisfy *d*: we take action *a* on desire *d* only where *d* is part of our *reason* for it. This suggests that it isn't enough for our desires to cohere with each other and to square with our needs. They and our beliefs and seeings together must compose a coherent fabric such that our acting on a reason sewn from that fabric doesn't frustrate our needs. That leads us back to our seeings. Yes, our seeings have to accord with how we want to be seeing things. But they also have to fit into a suitable total fabric.

How do our seeings "fit into" such a fabric? And how do beliefs and desires fit in? My suggestion will not be surprising. It is that they all fit together where the set all these compose *plus* our principles and our judgments passes a reflective-equilibrium test expanding on Goodman's above, where that test doesn't call for rejecting any of these beliefs, desires, or seeings – or any of the principles or judgments.[34] Say that your principles endorse the judgment that, if you believe *p* and want *q* and see some situation as *r*, you must also want *s*. Say that you have the belief and desire and seeing referred to in the antecedent but do *not* want *s*. Your beliefs, desires, and seeings, etc., don't all cohere; something has to go.

Still, our acting on our reasons (and thus on our seeings) must serve our needs. Doesn't this move us away from cohesion as the criterion of the rightness of seeings? Not if we make a distinction Anne herself makes at the end. She says, "I was perfectly right in being guided by [Lady Russell] . . . [but] I am not saying she did not err . . . [and I] never [w]ould . . . give such advice."[35] Why wouldn't Anne now give such advice if she was right back then to take it? Because she has learned that needs can't be ignored. She knows that some seeings that are right for a person are (we might say) not *grounded,* that they fit into no grounded fabric – no fabric that covers that person's needs. Rightness refers to cohesion alone; we can retain that idea. But we are free to look beyond rightness. Anne concluded we *must* look beyond it.

This lets us respond to the critic here too. The fit-together concept of rightness doesn't imply that anything goes, that we can see things however we like. It allows for the further constraint that seeings have to be grounded. But groundedness is about people's needs, which leads to the question of what a need *is,* and that is a murky question.[36] A need, it is said, is what is essential to some life project one has. A scholar needs access to books in this sense, a doctor needs a hospital, and all people need food and shelter. But why did Anne need Frederick; why did she need *just him*? To what life project was he essential? And what *is* a life project? I am left floundering here.[37]

5

SURPRISE AND SELF-KNOWLEDGE

HERE is a familiar puzzle. A teacher announces on Monday that there will be a surprise exam on either Wednesday or Friday. Her students reason as follows. Say that the teacher's announcement is true. Then, if the exam were on Friday, we would know by Thursday, and it wouldn't be a surprise. Therefore it won't be on Friday. This means it must be on Wednesday, and since we know that, it can't then surprise us. There can't be a surprise on either of these days. The teacher's announcement is false. It contradicts itself.

The teacher gives the exam on Friday and everyone is surprised. Where did the students go wrong? This has been much discussed, and I want to discuss it once more. I want then to extend my discussion to some larger issues.

1

Let me bring it down to just a single student's problem. The announcement can be put as five propositions. There will be an exam on either Wednesday or Friday:

(1) $W \vee F$

And it will come as a surprise to this student. If, that is, it will be on Wednesday, he won't, on Tuesday, believe it will be on Wednesday. And if it will be on Friday, he won't, on Thursday, believe it will be on Friday:

(2) $W \supset \sim B_t W$

(3) $F \supset \sim B_{th} F$[1]

Suppose also that

(4) $\sim(W \cdot F)$ and

(5) $\sim W \supset B_{th}{\sim}W$

These too are a part of what was announced.

Now suppose that the test will come Friday. This begins a conditional proof[2]:

(6)	F	
(7)	$\sim B_{th}F$	from (6) and (3)
(8)	$\sim W$	from (6) and (4)
(9)	$B_{th}{\sim}W$	from (8) and (5)

We want to proceed to $B_{th}F$, but (9) and (1) don't warrant that. What we need is (9) and $B_{th}(1)$. We are supposing (1), but that doesn't say that the student believes it – or will believe it on Thursday. So let us add the supposition that

(10) $B_{th}(1)$

This lets us move the proof to

(11) $B_{th}F$ (10) and (9)

which, by reductio, gives us

(12) $\sim F$ (11) and (7)

We go on to

(13) W (12) and (1) and

(14) $\sim B_t W$ (13) and (2)

These two lines say that the test will come Wednesday and will surprise the student. No contradiction here.

But suppose also that, on Tuesday, the student believes all our suppositions above:

(15) $B_t(1 \cdot 2 \cdot 3 \cdot 4 \cdot 5 \cdot 10)$

We then get

$$(16)\quad B_t W \qquad (15) \text{ and } (1) \text{ through } (13)$$

Here we do have a contradiction: (16) contradicts (14). But it doesn't follow that the teacher's announcement was false – this is where the students went wrong. What follows (by reductio) is that either that *or something else used in the argument* is false. That is, what follows is

$$(17)\quad \sim(1 \cdot 2 \cdot 3 \cdot 4 \cdot 5 \cdot 10 \cdot 15)$$

There is a tacit assumption above. We are assuming that the student's beliefs are deductively closed, that he believes the deductive consequences of the conjunction of all he believes. He is, in that sense, deductively *thorough*, and will continue being thorough until at least this Thursday.[3] Assume now also he is belief-*retentive*, that his beliefs are *stable*, stable at least until Thursday, barring new pertinent information – that he gives up no beliefs (before Thursday) unless he gets such information.[4] This allows us to simplify.

Let *m* be Monday, *today*. Then, because of belief retention, (15) can be replaced by

$$(15')\quad B_m(1 \cdot 2 \cdot 3 \cdot 4 \cdot 5 \cdot 10) \qquad \text{and also by}$$

$$(15'')\quad B_m(1 \cdot 2 \cdot 3 \cdot 4 \cdot 5)$$

for (15″) now implies (10), which thus becomes redundant. So (17) reduces to

$$(17')\quad \sim(1 \cdot 2 \cdot 3 \cdot 4 \cdot 5 \cdot 15'')$$

which is equivalent to

$$(18)\quad (1 \cdot 2 \cdot 3 \cdot 4 \cdot 5) \supset \sim B_m(1 \cdot 2 \cdot 3 \cdot 4 \cdot 5) \qquad \text{and to}$$

$$(19)\quad B_m(1 \cdot 2 \cdot 3 \cdot 4 \cdot 5) \supset \sim(1 \cdot 2 \cdot 3 \cdot 4 \cdot 5)$$

Nothing is wrong with the teacher's announcement, nor indeed with $1 \cdot 2 \cdot 3 \cdot 4 \cdot 5$; certainly the conjunction isn't contradictory. But there clearly *is* something wrong with $B_m(1 \cdot 2 \cdot 3 \cdot 4 \cdot 5)$. Let us describe someone who is deductively thorough and belief-retentive (during this period) as *disciplined.* We have assumed that the student is disciplined and have shown that, if $1 \cdot 2 \cdot 3 \cdot 4 \cdot 5$ is true, he doesn't believe it (this is (18)). Also – this says the same – that if he believes it, it isn't true (19). Strictly, he *can't* believe it, not in good logical conscience: there is no possible world in which he is disciplined *and* believes it *and* it is true.

Here is a simpler scenario. The teacher says there will be a surprise exam on Wednesday.[5] She tells the student that

(20) W   and

(21) $\sim B_t W$

No problem with $20 \cdot 21$; perhaps the exam *will* be on Wednesday and will surprise the student. But if

(22) $B_m(20 \cdot 21)$ then

(23) $B_t W$ (22)

Since (23) contradicts (21), it follows (by reductio) that

(24) $\sim(20 \cdot 21 \cdot 22)$ and so too that

(25) $(20 \cdot 21) \supset \sim B_m(20 \cdot 21)$ and

(26) $B_m(20 \cdot 21) \supset \sim(20 \cdot 21)$

Nothing is wrong with the announcement here either. Still, there is something wrong with (22). As with $1 \cdot 2 \cdot 3 \cdot 4 \cdot 5$, $20 \cdot 21$ is not contradictory, but the student can't properly believe it, for he would be believing a proposition that can be shown to be false if he believes it and is disciplined.[6] Jaakko Hintikka calls such propositions *doxastically indefensible* for this person.[7] I will call them *incredible* for him, or not properly *believable* by him – not believable in themselves, whatever else he believed. He cannot *properly* believe such a proposition because he could defend his believing it only by admitting to a lack of discipline. If he were disciplined (and he believed it), it would have to be false.

A person who believes what is logically false believes what must be false if he believes it (and also if he doesn't). What he believes must be false *whoever* believes it (or doesn't). This says that what is logically false is incredible for all. We have been speaking of incredible propositions that may in fact be true – the teacher's announcement is true! – and these are incredible for some people only. Thus 20 · 21 is incredible for the student but isn't so *for me,* there being nothing in that announcement about *my* being surprised. *I* can properly believe it, the student involved cannot. Getting beyond our scenarios: I can say of somebody else that this or that will surprise that person, but no one can say *about himself* (can properly believe) that *p* will surprise him.

Here is a further consequence. Again, 1 · 2 · 3 · 4 · 5 is incredible for the student but not for the teacher. She can properly believe it, though the student can't. Still, if she believes the student is disciplined and she herself is disciplined, she must believe (19), for (19) follows from what she believes. And if, besides, she believes he believes 1 · 2 · 3 · 4 · 5, she has to believe ~(1 · 2 · 3 · 4 · 5) – believing (19) and its antecedent, she has to believe its consequent. If she believes she convinced the student of the truth of the announcement she made, she must believe it is false! This brings out a new constraint: even if a proposition isn't incredible for you, you can't consistently believe that proposition along with believing that some (disciplined) person for whom it is incredible believes it.

Let me touch on three small points. Is the above about *surprise*? I held that *p* would surprise the student if he didn't believe it beforehand. Perhaps this put it poorly; perhaps a person is only surprised if, beforehand, he believed ~*p*. No problem in that for us here. We need just to stretch the concept of discipline to cover belief *consistency* (an idea taken for granted in the preceding paragraph), the idea of a person's not both believing p and believing $\sim p$.[8] Suppose that the teacher meant that her students would be surprised in the stronger sense. Changing her announcement to give it that meaning cannot weaken its force, this because the assumption of discipline lets us now move from $B{\sim}p$ to $\sim Bp$. So our conclusion would still stand. What the teacher said would still be incredible for the student.

Also, the student isn't surprised unless, in the end, when p comes true, he believes it is true. I left this unsaid above; to make it explicit, put $\mathrm{W} \supset ({\sim}B_{\mathrm{t}}\mathrm{W} \cdot B_{\mathrm{w}}\mathrm{W})$ and $\mathrm{F} \supset ({\sim}B_{\mathrm{th}}\mathrm{F} \cdot B_{\mathrm{f}}\mathrm{F})$ in place of (2) and (3) and put ${\sim}B_{\mathrm{t}}\mathrm{W} \cdot B_{\mathrm{w}}\mathrm{W}$ in place of (21). The lines that follow can be kept as they are.

Also, I speak of self-*knowledge*, but the above has brought out only that there are things about ourselves that we can't properly *believe*. This too is not a problem, for if we cannot believe them, we cannot know them either. We can't have full self-knowledge because we can't have full self-belief. We aren't fully knowable to ourselves because we aren't fully credible to ourselves.

2

The surprise exam conundrum is of no interest in itself. That is why I discussed it. I counted on no one's really caring how things came out in that situation to let the reader be receptive to my analysis of it. I want now to apply that analysis to a different situation.

My wife knows me very well. Still, she sometimes gets me wrong. Say that I am agonizing whether to do p or q, and she tells me the outcome is clear: I will choose to do p.[9]

I now think about this. She says that, on Wednesday, I will choose p. This p is indeed an option for me, and not just in the *could-do* sense, the sense that I *could* do p. It is a *decisional* option for me, one of the action-possibilities I am now considering, one of the set of those from which I want to choose. That means it is (*a*) an action I neither yet think I will take or that I won't. It is also (*b*) an action I think I would take if I chose it. So if I accepted my wife's prediction that I will choose *p*, I would (by *b*) now think I would take it. But then (by *a*) *p* wouldn't be an option, and neither would *q* be an option. There would be nothing for me to choose. So – aha! – she is wrong. She has contradicted herself! And I go on agonizing until, on Wednesday, I choose to do *p*. Her prediction turns out to be true; it was *not* contradictory. Where did my reasoning fail?

I will stand by *a* and *b*. A set of options composes an *issue*, and an issue is a situation it makes some sense to agonize over. There is no sense in agonizing where we know what we will do – for instance, in sweating out the question of whether or not to exhale. And it makes no sense to agonize where we doubt we would follow through. There is no point in Romeo's asking whether he ought to leave Juliet: he doubts he would leave her even if he chose to, so leaving her isn't an option for him. My *a* and *b* are not the problem.[10]

Where then did I go wrong? My wife predicted I would, on Wednesday, choose *p*; she predicted

(27) $C_W p$

Since what I choose must have been an option,[11]

(28) *p* will on Tuesday be an option for me (27), and

(29) $\sim B_t p$ (28), by a, and

(30) $B_t(C_W p \supset p)$ (28), by *b*

This alone is not troublesome. But if I accept my wife's prediction, if I believe it *now*, on Monday – if, that is,

(31) $B_m(27)$, then

(32) $B_t C_W p$ (31), and

(33) $B_t p$ (32) and (30)

Since (33) contradicts (29), something has to go. But nothing is wrong with (27); my thinking failed in faulting (27) alone. I should have concluded that

(34) $\sim(27 \cdot 31)$ and so too that

(35) $(27) \supset \sim B_{m}(27)$ and

(36) $B_{m}(27) \supset \sim(27)$

Suppose that I am disciplined.[12] Then, if (27) is true, I don't believe it – this is (35). And if I believe it, it isn't true – this is (36). My wife may be right to believe (27), but (27) isn't credible *for me*, for if I believe it, it has to be false (given that I am disciplined). A person can say about other people that they will choose certain options they have, but no one can say about himself, can properly believe, that he will choose *p*.

Let me stress the word "properly" here. We are free to believe what we please; I can believe that I will choose *p*, can *in fact* believe this. However, I can't believe it "in good logical conscience," since that calls for my not believing any proposition that my belief would make false (given that I am disciplined). Thus I can't *properly* believe I will choose *p*, cannot *properly* predict this.

We can't, in this sense, predict our own choices any more than we can our surprises. But this is not to be wondered at, for having chosen is like being surprised with *wanting* in place of *believing*. In choosing *p* we surprise ourselves (in the weaker sense of surprise), for, in choosing, we come to want what before we did not want. (This assumes a third condition of optionality *c*, that an option is an action we neither yet want or don't want to take.)

And there is more of the same. We can't predict our *learnings*. Say that you will come to learn *p*, say on this coming Wednesday. You can't learn what you already think is true (this corresponds to *a*), so you won't yet believe *p* on Tuesday. Still, you surely will then believe that whatever you learned would be true. (This corresponds to *b*.) No contradiction there, but if you *believe* that you will learn *p*, the argument continues as in (32) to (36). Thus your learning *p* on Wednesday is now incredible for you. Since the truth of *p* will surprise you, you can't predict your learning it. No one can properly believe he will learn (or discover, or realize) *p*.[13]

We can take this beyond prediction, beyond our foreknowledge (our fore*belief*) of our own choices and learnings. For if *p* isn't properly believable and *q* implies *p*, then *q* isn't believable either. Say that *r*, *s*, and *t* are your options, that *O* reports the outcomes of taking them in different possible contexts, that *P* is your probability distribution and *U* your utility distribution, and that you are rational (the last clause extends being disciplined). Let all this be *q*. Let *p* be that you will choose *r*, and say that *p* follows from *q*. Since *p* is not believable for you, neither is *q*. But *q* is not a proposition about any choice you will make, nor does it speak of anything else that will come to surprise you.

We can take it further still, beyond any connection with choosings or learnings. Say that you have forgotten *p*. You can't forget what is false, and can't forget *p* and also believe it, so *p* is true and you don't believe it. You cannot properly believe this conjunction (that *p* is true and you don't believe it) – that is like 20·21. And since the conjunction follows from your having forgotten *p*, your having forgotten *p* isn't believable for you either.[14]

Again, these are limits to *self*-belief and *self*-knowledge. *Other*-knowledge is not so restricted. Jill can know what Jack will choose. Still, she cannot pass that knowledge she has about him to Jack – such knowledge is out of bounds for him.[15] This reverses the usual thesis on people's mental privacy, that we can know about ourselves what no one else can unless we tell them (for instance, that we now have an itch). The point here is the opposite (and stronger), that other people can know things about us that we can't know even if they tell us. Privileged access goes in both directions.

To connect this with older ideas, suppose that

(37) Jack believes nothing

And suppose also that Jack believes this, that

(38) $B(37)$

Then it is false that Jack believes nothing,

(39) $\sim(37)$ (38)

This contradicts (37), so it follows that

(40) $\sim(37 \cdot 38)$ and also that

(41) $(37) \supset \sim B(37)$ and

(42) $B(37) \supset \sim(37)$

Jack may in fact be a total skeptic: (37) may be true. Jill can believe that Jack is a skeptic, but he himself can't rightly believe it, for he cannot rightly believe what must be false if he believes it.[16] As in the case of the famous Cretan (the one who said that he always lied), the moral has to do with self-reference. It is that certain propositions referring to a specified person x can't be properly believed by that person. If he believes them, they cannot be true. (*Jack believes nothing* cannot be true if Jack believes it. *He always lies* can be true even then, though it can't be true if he *says* it.) So also with our other cases; these too involve some x's believing some proposition referring to x. They too reveal the impropriety of certain beliefs that are self-referential.[17]

3

I can hear a question. OK, we can't predict our own choices, can't properly believe we will make them, but we can predict our *actions*. We can't predict that we will choose p, but we can predict we will *do* p: believing *that* is not improper. True, if we now believe we will do it, we can't go on to *choose p*. (By *a*, $C_t p \supset \sim B_m p$, so $B_m p \supset \sim C_t p$.) And, if we will choose *p*, we can't believe we will do *p*. But why should this concern us?

First, because it bears on the question of the limits of our knowledge of ourselves. Whatever we are going to choose, we can't ever know beforehand we will choose it – can't even properly *believe* we will choose it. Others may know, but we ourselves can't. To that extent, our knowledge is bounded, and bounded not by our physical limitations but by the logic of thought.[18]

This may leave you unconcerned, so here is a second point. Yes, we can deny ourselves the beliefs that I say are improper. We lose nothing of any importance where we avoid such beliefs. Still, we sometimes ascribe such beliefs both to ourselves and to others. Sometimes we even endorse some ideas that oblige us to do that. We then sometimes trip ourselves up, so it is well to look out against it.

Here is a case in which that would pay. Jack and Jill are in a Prisoners' Dilemma.[19] They can either cooperate or not – not cooperating is *defecting*. For each, defection is the dominant option; and, for Adam, the probabilities of Eve's acting thus or so are independent of his action, and correspondingly for Eve. Both Jack and Jill are rational, so they both will choose to defect. And since they both prefer the outcome of both cooperating to that of both defecting, they will both be sorry.

On the usual analysis, there is no way around this where they think they won't meet again.[20] But say that they think they will meet again, that their present interaction is only the first of many just like it. Here it may seem that the prospect each faces of having to live with the other's resentment ought to deter defection. Still, it often is argued that, where the number of rounds is finite and known to both agents and both are rational, both will choose to defect from the start to the finish.

The argument is this. Suppose that the number of rounds is known by both Jack and Jill to be 100, and that they both are rational. In the 100th, each will know that there will be no further meetings (and no resentment to worry about), so each will choose to defect. Let Jack think that Jill is rational and that she thinks the 100th round is the last. He will then think in the 99th that Jill will defect in the 100th whatever he does in the 99th, that his cooperating in the 99th round wouldn't be rewarded by Jill in the 100th. He will therefore defect in the 99th, and Jill, thinking likewise about Jack, will too.

The same in round 98; each expecting the other to defect in the round that follows, each will here choose to defect, though we here must also assume that Jack thinks Jill thinks *him* rational and must assume that Jill thinks he thinks *her* rational – and that each thinks the other thinks the 100th round is the last. So we move stepwise back to round 1 (with more luggage at each prior stage), both parties defecting all the way.

This backward induction rests on assumptions about these people's beliefs about each other. Often the assumptions are said to be these: both Jack and Jill believe that they both are rational (that they will be throughout), and believe that, in each round, they will face a Prisoners' Dilemma and that there will be 100 rounds. Both also believe that they both believe this, that both believe they both believe it, that both believe they both believe they both believe it, etc. – though the full strength of this last condition isn't needed in every round. All of that together is the *Common Belief Assumption* (*CB*), strictly: the assumption of the commonality of their beliefs in their both being rational and about the structure of their interaction.

But if both Jack and Jill are disciplined, CB ascribes improper beliefs, beliefs that, if held, would be false. By CB, Jack now believes that in the 100th round he will be in a Prisoners' Dilemma and will there be rational and so choose to defect: he now believes $C_{100}d$. Applying the argument from (31), we can show that $B_1(C_{100}d) \supset \sim C_{100}d$, and since Jack now believes $C_{100}d$ (and is disciplined), $C_{100}d$ is false. By CB and the backward induction, Jack also believes $C_{99}d$ and $C_{98}d$ and $C_{97}d \ldots$, and so we can likewise show that $C_{99}d$ is false, and also $C_{98}d$ and $C_{97}d$ ... Jill too believes $C_{100}d$, and $C_{99}d$, and $C_{98}d$ ..., and so these propositions (about *her*) are false too. Given that Jack and Jill are disciplined, all this follows from CB alone. This means that either CB is false or that both Jack and Jill hold beliefs that, being improper, are false – in which case neither Jack nor Jill will choose defection in any round.

One could say that CB is true and that neither will choose to defect but that they always *will* defect, and that the backward induction leads them to that conclusion. The fact would remain that, by CB, a backward induction leads them also – and us too – to false conclusions about what they will *choose*. It implies they both will choose to defect in every round x, that, for every x, $C_x d$. Call this conclusion r. And, again, it implies that, for every x, $B_1(C_x d)$, that each *believes* he will there choose to defect. We know that, by discipline, for every x, $B_1(C_x d) \supset {\sim}C_x d$, which yields s: for every x, ${\sim}C_x d$. Either r or s must be false.[21] Since a sound argument cannot lead us from true premises to false conclusions, CB has to go.[22]

To save the backward induction, we can make use of a weaker thesis, one that, unlike CB, ascribes (imposes) no improper beliefs. Let S be a set of propositions reporting the parties as being rational and the structure of their interaction. Suppose that each party believes every item in S that he (she) can *properly* believe (in our special sense of *propriety*), that each believes the other believes the items *that other* can properly believe, that each believes the other believes the same of *him* (of *her*), etc. Call this the *Reciprocal Belief Assumption* (*RB*), strictly: the assumption of the reciprocity of their *proper* beliefs regarding the items in S. (CB with regard to these items implies RB with regard to them, but not vice versa.)

Where S reports the situation of Jack and Jill described at the start, RB implies that Jack believes that Jill is rational (plus other facts about her). It implies that Jill believes that Jack is rational (plus other facts about *him*). It implies that Jack believes that Jill believes that Jack is rational, that Jill believes that Jack believes that Jill is rational, etc. It does *not* imply that either believes that he (she) himself (herself) is rational. Nor does it imply that either believes of himself (herself) that he (she) will choose to defect in round 100, or in round 99, or. . . . No improprieties here. But note that what this leaves us suffices for the backward induction, for the *outside observer's* prediction of the parties choosing to defect every time.[23] The observer's backward induction doesn't call for CB. It needs only the weaker RB – and the observer/predictor's beliefs about both parties being rational, etc.[24]

This thinking can be extended. CB is often said to be essential to the theory of games, or at least to justifications of equilibrium solutions. If that were right, it would mean trouble, for then such solutions could be justified only where (as above) the players hold false beliefs about what they are going to choose. I suggest it is wrong, that CB is more than game theory needs, that the jobs it is asked to do can be done by RB. Ken Binmore and Adam Brandenburger say that "any equilibrium notion that incorporates some measure of self-prophesying necessarily entails common [belief] requirements. . . ."[25] I am saying that equilibrium analysis provides just for *other*-prophesying, that a player isn't also (can't be!) the observer/*predictor* of the game. The message here is the same as in the Prisoners' Dilemma: the logic of proper belief denies us nothing that we need, but going against that logic sometimes undermines what we say.

That message is not one for game theory only, for CB sometimes figures in other contexts too. John Rawls, presenting a theory of justice, proposes what he calls a *publicity* condition. Initially, he speaks of that in connection with a system of rules: "A person taking part in an institution knows what the rules demand of him and of the others. He also knows that the others know this and that they know that he knows this, and so on."[26] Still, he later goes beyond rules: "I shall suppose that the parties [behind a "veil of ignorance"] possess all general information."[27] Their all having that information is then itself a general datum, and so they have to believe *that*, etc.

For Rawls, this means that, behind the veil, each person knows that everyone there – including himself – has p and q and... as options, options of distributing certain goods in certain specified ways,[28] that everyone prefers more goods to less, and that everyone is maximining-rational (and is ignorant of his own place in society, of his current advantages and disadvantages over others). If everyone knew this about everyone involved, everyone would know it about himself and so could predict how he himself would choose, which we have seen isn't logically possible for any disciplined person.

No problem here for Rawls, for he retreats from the publicity condition, though only on the grounds of the "complexity" of some of the information behind the veil. I am saying there are *logical* grounds for backing off from publicity, from CB-publicity; that if Rawls in fact assumed it, he would undermine his theory of justice, his theory of just distributions. Fortunately, he doesn't need it. He doesn't need to suppose that people behind the veil are that well-informed. (He doesn't even need the weaker, RB-sort of publicity.)

Again, there is no purpose for which we need to hold improper beliefs, and none for which we must suppose that other people hold any. But we sometimes ascribe such beliefs to ourselves or to others, and that can mess up our thinking. So it pays to keep the logic of proper belief in mind.

4

Let me remark on some ramifications. We have spoken of the skeptic who believes nothing whatever. He can't believe this about himself – can't *properly* believe it – for if he believed it, it wouldn't be true. Consider now his sister, who has joined a cult that requires its members not to *want* anything. Can she want to comply with that? If she wanted not to want anything, her wanting this would defeat what she wants: she then *would* want something (for she would want *that*). I will say she can't *properly* want it.

Take also the teacher who announces to her students that there will be a test on Wednesday and that its being on that day will be a disappointment to them. This means there will be a test on Wednesday and that the students will want beforehand, say on Tuesday, that it *not* be on Wednesday. Can the students want that disappointment? Can people ever want to be disappointed by a specified *p*?

Being disappointed by *p* is this, that *p* is true (and you know it) but you wanted ~*p*.[29] I have argued that no one can properly believe he will be surprised by *p*. Recall the remarks about surprise in its stronger sense – a parallel argument (with *wanting* in place of *believing*) shows that no one can properly want to be disappointed by *p*. If he will be disappointed by it, he doesn't want that disappointment, and if he wants the disappointment, he will not be disappointed (by *p*).[30] Just as we can't predict our surprises, so we can't hope for our disappointments.

Could we press this analysis further? Think of the ethics of Kant. Kant presented a formal criterion of the desires we could morally act on. His Categorical Imperative is this: "Act only on that maxim whereby you can at the same time will that it should become a universal law."[31] For Kant, the *maxim* of an action we consider taking is the desire to do what we see (what we *understand*) we would be doing in that action. The maxim is the desire on which the agent acts,[32] so we might put it more simply like this – in terms of allowing for *desire* commonality – that no one ought ever to act on a desire that couldn't be held by all.[33] Still, this has no force whatever, for any desire could be held by all.

But perhaps that sells Kant short. Perhaps he means that the maxim you act on must be one that could be held by all people *who are logically disciplined*. This would move us to an idea of allowing for desire-*reciprocity*,[34] and to this different version of the Imperative, that no one ought ever to act on a desire that couldn't be *properly* held by all. If Jill couldn't properly want p true, Jack oughtn't to act on his wanting p. This again uses "properly" in our special, logical sense – for Kant, morality rests wholly on logic. (The Imperative itself isn't logic, but when it is put in terms of propriety, what it excludes depends just on logic.)

Here is an appealing corollary: never act on any desire to disappoint someone by p. We are led to this by the fact that whoever you want to disappoint can't properly want to be disappointed by it. (The fact emerges in the proof of the impropriety of his wanting that, so the "fact" is logic.) This doesn't exclude your disappointing others. It says you ought never to *act on the maxim* of disappointing someone by p, that you may never *set your mind* on that, may not *determine* to disappoint. Are there other such corollaries? There are if we move a step further.

We have taken disciplined people to be consistent both belief-wise and desire-wise.[35] Let me suggest that being disciplined also calls for consistency in one's beliefs and desires together, that if disciplined Jill believes p, she does not want $\sim p$.[36] Suppose she now falsely believes p. And suppose that she *wants* (*D*: *desires*) this – that she *wants* to falsely believe p. Here we have

(43) $\sim p \cdot Bp$ and

(44) $D(43)$

By desire-thoroughness, we have

(45) $D\sim p$ (44) and

(46) $Bp \cdot D\sim p$ (45) and (43)

Since by belief-and-desire-consistency, (46) is false, we have, by reductio,

(47) $\sim(43 \cdot 44)$ and also

(48) $(43) \supset \sim D(43)$ and

(49) $D(43) \supset \sim(43)$

These last lines say that Jill can't properly want herself to be wrong about *p*. (They say that, if she wanted to be wrong, she *wouldn't* be wrong; this is (49).) Since she can't properly want (43), the Categorical Imperative implies that Jack ought not to act on *his* wanting it: on his desire that she be wrong about *p*. He oughtn't to try to mislead her. In that sense, he oughtn't to *lie* to her. Kant would have said this is pay dirt. To lie is to act on a maxim-*to-deceive*, and Kant insisted that no one may lie – he held that an action taken on a maxim-to-deceive is immoral. Those who agree with that idea can take this last proof as a vindication of Kant. Those who *dis*agree can take it as a reductio of the Categorical Imperative, of the injunction to follow reciprocity, to never act on any desire that couldn't be properly held by all.

6

THE LOGIC OF AMBIGUITY

WE will start with the mother topic, with the logic of thought. That is not the logic of truth; it isn't about validity and about what follows from what. It has to do with what a person ought to believe or not to believe, or with what he ought (or oughtn't) to believe if he believes certain other matters. Also with what he ought to *want* or not to want. . . . Most broadly: with what *propositional attitudes* he ought to hold or not to hold, or to hold or not hold in certain contexts of others.

1

First, about belief. There are said to be some people who believe nothing whatever. No logical fault in being a skeptic. We may think such people foolish, or excessively cautious, but we can't call them illogical.

Suppose that Jack is a skeptic, that

(1) Jack believes nothing

No problem there. But suppose too he *believes* he is a skeptic, that he believes (1), that

(2) $B(1)$

It follows (by the usual logic of truth) that

(3) Jack believes *some*thing from (2)[1]

This contradicts (1), and so, by reductio, it follows that

(4) $\sim(1 \cdot 2)$ and also

(5) $(2) \supset \sim(1)$ which says that

(6) $B(1) \supset \sim(1)$

Jack is a skeptic; nothing wrong there. But if he *believes* he is a skeptic, what he believes can be shown to be false (as in (6)). If we describe a belief as false where it focuses on a false proposition, Jack's belief then makes itself false. In that sense, it undermines itself, and there is something wrong in that.

Here is a second situation.[2] Suppose that *p* but Jack doesn't believe it. This is

(7) $p \cdot \sim Bp$

And suppose that Jack believes (7), that

(8) $B(p \cdot \sim Bp)$

Let Jack be *logically disciplined*: let his thinking accord with logic. Or let him just be *deductively thorough* – let him believe the deductive consequences of the conjunction of all he believes. That lets us move to

(9) Bp from (8)

This contradicts (7), so it follows that $\sim(7 \cdot 8)$, that

(10) $\sim(p \cdot \sim Bp \cdot B(p \cdot \sim Bp))$ which is equivalent to

(11) $B(p \cdot \sim Bp) \supset \sim(p \cdot \sim Bp)$

Nothing wrong with Jack's not believing *p*. But if he *believes* the conjunction of *p* and of his not believing it, then (if he is deductively thorough) what he believes can be shown to be false. The belief he here has undermines itself – or perhaps better, Jack is self-undermining.

There is more to logical discipline than mere deductive thoroughness. Let us assume that Jack is *consistent*, that, if he believes *x*, he doesn't believe $\sim x$, whatever *x* might be.[3] This gives us a closely related proof. In place of (7) and (8), we start now with

(12) $p \cdot B{\sim}p$ and

(13) $B(p \cdot B{\sim}p)$

Consistency calls for

(14) ${\sim}(Bp \cdot B{\sim}p)$ which is equivalent to

(15) $B{\sim}p \supset {\sim}Bp$

We also have

(16) Bp (13), by thoroughness, and

(17) ${\sim}Bp$ (15) and (12)

Since (17) contradicts (16), it follows that ${\sim}(12 \cdot 13)$, that

(18) ${\sim}(p \cdot B{\sim}p \cdot B(p \cdot B{\sim}p))$ which is equivalent to

(19) $B(p \cdot B{\sim}p) \supset {\sim}(p \cdot B{\sim}p)$

What it comes to is this: that if Jack believes (7), what he believes is false; and so too if he believes (12). (This assumes he is disciplined.) And if he believes (1), that he is a skeptic, he *isn't* (whether he is disciplined or not). It may be that (1) and (7) and (12) are in fact all true. Jack may in fact be a skeptic, etc. And if Jill believes these items, there is no problem for her. However, if *Jack* believes them (and is disciplined), he believes what he can't believe without undermining himself, so he can't *properly* believe them. We will refer to propositions as *not properly believable* for a person where, if that person believed them (and were disciplined), they would have to be false. We might speak of them too as *unconditionally* unbelievable for him, or as *incredible* for him. (Again, they might be incredible *for Jack* but not incredible *for Jill*.)

We will also speak of *reflection*: a reflective person believes no proposition he cannot properly believe. He holds no beliefs that are self-undermining. Also, he doesn't *dis*believe the negations of propositions not believable for him – he doesn't believe those negations false. Thus, if Jack is reflective, he believes neither (7) nor (12). And he doesn't disbelieve either

(20) $p \supset Bp$, the negation of (7)

or

(21) $p \supset \sim B \sim p$, the negation of (12)

or

(22) $\sim Bp \supset B \sim Bp$, which corresponds to (20), after $\sim Bp$ is put for p in (7)–(11)

or

(23) $Bp \supset p$, which corresponds to (21), after $\sim p$ is put for p in (12)–(19)[4]

or

(24) $B(p \supset q) \supset (Bp \supset Bq)$, this because (24) follows from $B\sim$(24) where the agent is disciplined,[5] and thus, by definition, $\sim$(24) isn't properly believable for him

or

(25) t, where t is any tautology, this because t follows from $B \sim t$ (it follows from every proposition), and thus, by definition, $\sim t$ isn't properly believable (for anyone!)

The last few lines are of special interest because the four theses (22)–(25) define the modal system S5 – or rather, that system applied to belief.[6] So it follows that a reflective person is committed to that modal system in this weak, negative sense, that he can't *dis*believe these theses (where the *B*'s are *his* beliefs), that he cannot disbelieve that (22)–(25) are true of himself. Could we now strengthen this? Could we show he must *believe* these theses? Only if we could establish that if he doesn't *dis*believe x (doesn't believe $\sim x$), he must believe x – or could strengthen reflection to say that if he cannot *properly* believe $\sim x$, he must believe x. But there is nothing wrong with believing neither $\sim x$ nor x, with suspending judgment (even where $\sim x$ can't be properly believed). Thus we cannot get beyond a reflective person's *dis*believing these theses.

2

The above has been only about belief, but all that it rests on regarding belief is that a disciplined person's beliefs are both thorough and consistent and that a person who is reflective believes only what he can properly believe. So it carries over to other propositional attitudes of which the same might be said.

Think of *wantings* (*desirings*). Let us say that a disciplined person *wants* the deductive consequences of the conjunction of all he wants and that, if he wants x, he doesn't want $\sim x$. This gives us proofs like those just above, with D (for *desire*) in place of B. Say that p isn't properly *wantable* for a person where, if he wanted p (and were disciplined), p would have to be false[7] – that it isn't properly wantable where his wanting it would be self-undermining. Also, that a reflective person wants no propositions that aren't wantable for him, and doesn't want their negations false. It follows that $p \supset Dp$ isn't wanted-false by him, nor is $p \supset \sim D \sim p$, nor are the D-analogues of (22)–(25), the S5 logic applied to desires.

Our principles of discipline and of reflection can't be extended to every attitude. They get no handle on attitudes tokened by several propositions jointly, no handle, for instance, on preferences. (Two tokening items there: we prefer *p* to *q*.) Nor do they extend to every attitude that is tokened by one at a time. Neither thoroughness nor consistency holds for probability settings. If you set a probability of .6 on $p \cdot q$, you needn't also set it on *p*. And if you set probability .5 on *p*, you may (you must!) also set it on $\sim p$.[8]

Does an S5 logic hold for *hopes* and *fears* and the like? The answer depends on whether our principles of discipline hold for these attitudes. Also on whether we ought to guard against their being self-undermining. (If you fear *p* and that is self-undermining, your fearing it implies $\sim p$. Should your fearing it put you at ease?) Also on how far we take "and the like." Is being ashamed that *p* a tokened propositional attitude? Is having learned *p* in school? If *yes*, must a logic of thought apply there?

Let us put these questions aside and turn to people's *seeings*, to how people cope with ambiguity, how they *dis*ambiguate. I have argued that how we see things figures in all of our thinking, and that seeings can't be ignored where we ask whether a certain thinking is logical.[9] So a general logic of thought has to attend to seeings.

This brings up a problem right off. I have said that the logic of thought has to do with our propositional attitudes, with those that we ought (or oughtn't) to have and those we ought to move to from others. But I have also said that our seeings aren't propositional attitudes.[10] You may see your living where you do as *I live at home* or *I live with my parents* or *I live cheaply. . . . What* you see is that situation; you *see it as* this or that proposition. Seeings are *situational* attitudes, though the way we see situations is identified propositionally. How then can a logic of thought attend to the seeings we have?

It can do that by making use of the converse concept here. To see a situation *s* as a certain proposition *p* is to take *p* as what is *salient* in *s*, what is salient in it *for us*, what stands out or *leaps* out at us ("salient" is from the Latin for leaping). Better, it is to *make p* salient of *s*. Let us put it this way, that it is to *make p salient of the situation that p reports*. Making *p* salient of that situation – most briefly: *making p salient* – is a *p*-tokened propositional attitude. Thus making-salient falls within the scope of our logic.

But how can a seeing be the same as a making-salient? How can a single state of mind be both a situational and a propositional attitude? Compare that question to this: how can Jack's being drawn to Jill be a two-term relation and his being drawn to his best friend's wife a three-term relation? (Jill *is* his best friend's wife.) It can be both because what we call it depends on how we structure or *see* it. So too with how an attitude can be both situational and propositional. To say it is both is only to say that we can parse it either way, that we can, on different occasions, see it (our *having* it) differently.

Every situation can be differently seen, even that of our seeing *s* as *p*. How *should* that seeing be seen? That depends on the context. In most cases, it doesn't matter, and we can see our seeings *as seeings* (as situational attitudes). Where we are trying to fit people's seeings into a general logic of thought, we have to see them as salience-makings (as *propositional* attitudes).

Is the logic of making-salient like that of belief? This raises several questions. Do the principles of discipline for salience and for belief correspond? Also, ought no one to make any proposition salient that, if he did (and were disciplined), would then have to be false? And, if we endorse that principle, are the propositions he can't properly make salient the analogues of those he can't properly believe? We will put off these matters to the end.

3

What logical principles should we accept? Should we accept those cited above, and which others should we accept? Also, what warrants a *should* in this context? What endorses our principles?

There is not much to go on here. Some writers have argued that keeping to certain principles assures us in the long run of certain desirable outcomes, if these can be had at all, or assures us (even in the short run) of avoiding undesirable ones. Such so-called *pragmatic* arguments have been given in support of induction, of expectedness maximization, of the principles of probability, and of some principles of preference. They are ingenious arguments and have been worked out in great detail, but it appears that none of them work.[11]

Other writers have held that some principles need no support or endorsement, that we *must* adhere to them, or must if our mental operations are to count as thinking at all; they hold that some principles are *a priori*,[12] or that some report innate, hard-wired constraints on our thinking.[13] But none of the principles here at issue are either *a priori* or hard-wiring reports. All are rules that might be questioned. All have sometimes been violated. And there are people who dismiss them, some of these people even promoting certain alternatives to them. If some people find it possible to reject a certain principle, it should be possible for those who retain it to say why they keep themselves to it.

The only course that has any promise looks to the cohesion of our principles and our judgments. This appears in its basic form in Nelson Goodman's concept of *reflective equilibrium*: "... [principles] and [judgments] alike are justified by being brought into agreement with each other. A [principle] is amended if it yields a [judgment] we are unwilling to accept; a [judgment] is rejected if it violates a [principle] we are unwilling to amend."[14]

Our topic is the *endorsement* of principles, not the "rejection" or "amendment" of them, so this has to be edited. Also, the line that Goodman is taking slights the holism here. We can't just say that a principle is endorsed if it imposes ("yields") a judgment we are willing to make. Judgments often are imposed only by several principles jointly. (The judgment that Jack ought not to believe (12) is imposed only by *B*-thoroughness and *B*-consistency and *B*-reflection together.) Sometimes too some principles impose a judgment we are willing to make along with others we are not. We have to say something like this: a *set of* principles is accepted (endorsed) if it imposes just such judgments as we are willing to make, and we are willing to make a certain judgment if it is imposed by a set of principles we are willing to accept.

This still does not take in enough. I accept *B*-thoroughness (with a proviso to come). Where *q* follows from *p*, that principle imposes the judgment that, *if* he believes *p*, Jack must believe *q*. Where I believe he does believe *p*, I will hold too that he must believe *q* – dropping the antecedent. This latter judgment is not imposed by the set of my principles alone but by that plus my belief about Jack. My refusal to make the judgment needn't discredit *B*-thoroughness.

So let us say that, in a reflective equilibrium, what we balance is a set of our principles and our judgments *and* our beliefs (e.g., my belief that Jack believes *p*). This now means that a set of principles is accepted if, *given our beliefs*, it imposes just such judgments as we are willing to make.[15] And that we are willing to make a certain judgment if, again, *given our beliefs*, it is imposed by a set of principles we are willing to accept. In the case above (a case of my refusing to make a certain judgment), where I retain my belief about Jack, I must give up *B*-thoroughness. Where I give up that belief, *B*-thoroughness can stay.

Some endorsed sets of principles may be *better* endorsed than others, this where the set of the willing judgments imposed (given . . .) by the set of principles P_1 contains all those imposed by P_2 (again, given . . .) and some others besides. Note too that set *P* may be endorsed where some more inclusive set isn't. In such cases, the smaller set (plus . . .) imposes only judgments we are willing to make, the larger set (plus . . .) also imposing judgments we refuse to make.

It may be argued that our equilibria can't be wholly comprehensive, that we cannot have a test of all our logical principles together, this because what imposes a judgment only imposes it *given some logic* – given some principles specifying what is implied by what.[16] And we can't just add these principles to the set of those being tested, for that would call for still other principles to warrant the claim that the judgment is imposed (imposed then by the larger set). The set of the principles the test endorses can't be the set of all those we accept.[17]

The logic of implication speaks of what has to be true if *this* or *that* is true: it is the logic *of truth*. Wherever we reflect on some possible judgment, on whether we are committed to it, we take some principles of that logic for granted. So, yes, the principles the test endorses can't be the set of all those we accept. Still, it can be the set of our principles of the logic *of thought* – of what a person ought (or oughtn't) to believe or to want or.... Our principles of what is implied by what, of the logic of truth, are not among these, so we are begging no question in appealing *to them* in our test.

4

We can now finally turn to particular principles of the logic of thought. We want to be getting to salience, to the logic of ambiguity, but let us move to that indirectly.

First, deductive *B*-thoroughness. This implies that a person who believes p has much else to believe: he must believe $p \vee q$ and also $p \vee q \vee r$ and also $p \vee q \vee r \vee s \ldots$, however distant to his mind these disjunctions are. A person who isn't a total skeptic must believe more than he ever believes – more than he *could* believe. Are we willing to make that judgment?

I am not willing to make it, this because, on my understanding, the "must" just above is directive. If someone *must* believe this or that, he can be faulted if he does not. And we cannot fault a person for not believing what he couldn't believe.[18]

I will suppose he needn't believe what he never has entertained, never in any way brought to mind, the *entertaining* of propositions being itself a propositional attitude, the minimal propositional attitude, the one implied by every other (*Bp* implies *Ep*, *Dp* implies *Ep*, etc.).[19] And I will give up *B*-thoroughness in favor of a principle of beliefs-and-entertainings – call it *B,E*-thoroughness. This calls only for our believing the *entertained* consequences of the conjunction of what we believe, those entertained *by us*.[20] (Say that *q* follows from some *p* we believe but that we don't now entertain *q* and thus do not believe it. Perhaps we are *wrong* not to entertain *q*. But the case for that will have to rest on more than that *q* follows from *p*.)

Likewise with simple *D*-thoroughness; this has to give way to *D,E*-thoroughness, to our only having to want the *entertained* consequences of the conjunction of what we want. It may be argued against *D,E*-thoroughness (and *has* been argued against *D*-thoroughness) that a person who wants *p* can't be required to want $p \vee q$ – not even this two-way disjunction, not even if he entertains it – because he may want $\sim q$, in which case $p \vee q$ could be made true (by *q*) without his being gratified. This assumes that, if we want $p \vee q$, its coming true must gratify us, and that idea won't stand. Being gratified is being pleased by something we wanted to happen and did, but only where we see what has happened as we expected to see it.[21] (You want a promotion. Your boss, an old friend, is fired and you are given his job. Does your promotion now gratify you?) If we want $p \vee q$ and expect to see the situation reported by that as *p*, we will *not* be gratified where *q* turns out true and we then see the situation reported by $p \vee q$ as *q*.

We have a second sort of holism here. The first was that we must assess our principles and judgments jointly (this was Goodman's point), and indeed assess our principles and judgments *and beliefs* jointly. Thus our principles are endorsed only all together, as a set. The second holism is that most principles govern judgments about several attitudes jointly – in the case of *D,E*-thoroughness, judgments about wanting *and* entertaining, about which propositions we now entertain we must want if we want certain others.

There are many such plural-attitude principles. One is that of *D,B*-consistency: if you believe x, you can't want $\sim x$. (This may be too strong and might be done without.) Another is that of *D,B*-thoroughness: if you believe x and you want y, and if z follows from $x \cdot y$ and neither x nor any conjunctive component of x follows from z, you must also want z.[22, 23] (We will have to qualify this as we did *B*-thoroughness above – by moving to *D,B,E*-thoroughness, by adding the proviso that z is *entertained*.)

Here are two more that reach very far – call them *extensionality* principles. The first is that of *D,B*-extensionality. This has to do with the holding of certain desires and beliefs together; it says that if you believe that x and y are coreportive propositions (that they report the same situation), you must either want them both or want neither. The second is that of *U,B*-extensionality; this says that if you believe that x and y are coreportive, you must set the same *utility* value on them. These are two principles I don't accept.[24]

Consider Orwell's Spanish Civil War story.[25] Orwell recalls being about to shoot a fascist soldier and realizing he would shoot a "fellow creature." He wanted p: *I shoot that fascist* but didn't want q: *I shoot that fellow creature*, though he knew that p and q were coreportive. By *D,B*-extensionality, he ought to have wanted either both or neither. I don't fault Orwell for wanting just p, and so am not willing to make that judgment. (Better perhaps, my declining to fault him *is* my refusal to make that judgment.) And so I can't accept the principle that, *inter alia*, imposes that judgment.

Or say that you are offered a gift and learn that the gift is a bribe. You want p: *I accept that gift* but don't want q: *I accept that bribe*, though you know that p and q are coreportive. By *D,B*-extensionality, you ought to want either both or neither.

Again, I don't go along with this. Yes, *p* and *q* report the same, the same situation *s*, but what we value – what we here *want* – are not situations but propositions. And I won't fault your wanting *p* (or *s*-under-*p*) and not wanting *q* (or *s*-under-*q*). This too now keeps me from accepting *D, B*-extensionality.

How can values that aren't extensional provide any guidance for choice and for action? Let us put that aside for a while and consider *D, B-expectedness*, a principle of outcome logic, of what you expect your action would *do*. This says that if you believe that *y* reports the outcome of what is reported by *x* and you want *y*, you must also want *x*. Should we accept this principle? Say that you want to get rich. You know (you *believe*) you are in your uncle's will and that your killing him would make you rich (and you know of no further outcome). The principle imposes the judgment that you must want to kill him. Should we accept this judgment?

I would say *that depends*. It depends on matters that are being left unmentioned, on how you *see* what in killing him you would do, on what is salient in that for you. If you make salient *In killing my uncle, I would make myself rich*, I accept it: you must want to kill him. (Only a thug would see it so, but that is not a point of logic.) If you make salient *In killing him, I would kill a nice, kindly old man* (or . . . *my mentor* or . . . *my mother's brother*), I reject it, for that connects what you might do with no proposition you now want to make true. Thus I reject mere *D, B*-expectedness and accept this *D, B, S*-principle instead, that if you believe that *y* reports the outcome of what is reported by *x* and you want *y* – and you make salient *In x'ing, I would y*[26] – you must also want *x*.

A similar *S*-clause qualification must be added to *D, B, E*-thoroughness. This then gives way to this *D, B, S*-principle, that if you believe *x* and you want *y*, and if *z* follows from $x \cdot y$ and neither *x* nor any conjunctive component of *x* follows from *z* – and you make salient *In z'ing, I would y* – you must also want *z*.[27] (Orwell knew that, in shooting that fascist, he would shoot that fellow creature, and he wanted to shoot that fascist, but *In shooting that fellow creature, I would shoot that fascist* wasn't salient for him. What was salient for him? Orwell suggests it was *In shooting that fellow, I would shoot someone like me.*)

We have at last come to some salience principles, though only to some in which making-salient is one of several attitudes covered. Here are two more such principles, both of them expectedness principles. In presenting *D, B, S*-expectedness, we supposed you were fully certain of the outcome of the action reported by x. Suppose now that you aren't, but that you know (believe) that y_1 reports the outcome of that action in context c_1, that y_2 reports its outcome in $c_2, \ldots$ and y_n its outcome in c_n, and that $c_1, c_2, \ldots c_n$ are pairwise exclusive and jointly exhaustive. Say that $u_1, u_2, \ldots u_n$ are the utilities you set on $y_1, y_2, \ldots y_n$, and that $p_1, p_2, \ldots p_n$ are the probabilities you set on c_1 given x, on c_2 given $x, \ldots$ and on c_n given x. A familiar *U, P, B*-expectedness principle is that you must set on x the utility $u_x = p_1u_1 + p_2u_2 + \cdots + p_nu_n$.

Does this serve its purpose? Say that you and Jack and Jill are lost in the jungle and they both are sick. You have medicine only for one; whoever gets it will recover, the other person will die. You have a coin you might toss. Still, Jill is a friend and Jack is a stranger – you would rather that Jill survived. How does *U, P, B*-expectedness apply? What utility ought you to set on your helping Jill?[28]

Let h be *I help Jill*; let t be *I let the coin-toss decide*. There are two contingencies: c_1 and c_2, heads and tails. If you make salient α: *In helping Jill, I would save a friend's life in* c_1 and α': *[the same] . . . in* c_2, u_h may be greater for you (by *U,P,B-expectedness*) than it would be if you made salient β: *In helping Jill, I would play God in* c_1 and β': *[the same] . . . in* c_2.[29] Likewise, if you make β and β' salient, u_h may be *lower* than it would be if you made α and α' salient. What is the utility you should set on h? I suggest that this depends on what you are making salient, on whether that is α and α' or β and β' or some other propositions. (Utility extensionality is *not* being imposed.) Thus I hold that *U,P,B*-expectedness isn't fully directive. It has to give way to *U,P,B,S*-expectedness – or U^+-expectedness for short – the *U,P,B*-principle with the qualification that you make salient *In x'ing, I would* y_1 *in context* $c_1, \ldots$ *would* y_2 *in* $c_2, \ldots$ and … *would* y_n *in* c_n.[30, 31]

Finally, *D,U,P,B,S*-expectedness – or D^+-expectedness. This is the idea that you must want one of those of your options which, in your view of them, has a maximal U^+-expectedness utility, a U^+-utility than which none has a greater. In the Jack-and-Jill medicine case, helping Jill and tossing a coin are your only real options. (Helping Jill dominates helping Jack, so you excluded the latter from the start.) If you see them solely in terms of saving (or *not* saving) the life of a friend, u_h is likely to be greater for you than u_t and you have to want *h*. If you see them in terms of playing (or not playing) God, u_t may be greater than u_h and you then have to want *t*. (Which way *ought* you to see them? The logic we have doesn't say.)[32]

I should note that none of these principles require that we hold any propositional attitudes. They require only that we hold this attitude or that *if* we hold certain others (and that we never hold any attitudes that would be self-undermining). They don't require that we believe or want *x* but only that we believe or want *x if*. . . . And they don't require any particular utility settings but only (in U^+-expectedness) that we set certain utilities *if*. . . . This means that, *a fortiori*, they don't require a utility distribution that, for every *x* and *y*, either sets a greater utility on one than on the other or sets the same on both: they don't require a distribution that is *complete*. Adopting our principles doesn't commit us to supposing the commensurability of all utility settings (nor, again, commit us to any settings whatever).[33]

As for U^+- and D^+-expectedness, we don't even need a complete distribution to *apply* these principles. All we need is a distribution – in the case of D^+-expectedness, we need one for each set of options – over the various *y*'s in our salient *In x'ing, I would* y_1 *in* c_1, ... *would* y_2 *in* c_2, ... and ... *would* y_n *in* c_n. (These utilities need not be commensurate with those that we set in other distributions on other propositions.) Such a restricted utility distribution is in fact often made. That is, in many choice situations, we indeed see the outcomes in ways for which we have a utility metric – perhaps in terms of the money-yield of these outcomes, or the lives they would save, or the jobs they would generate.... So our expectedness principles often have applications. Still, the mere *adoption* of them doesn't even call for our having such a restricted distribution. It requires only that *if* we have one....

5

Two issues have been left open. First, we have spoken of salience principles that are principles of several attitudes together, salience being among them. Are there any principles of salience alone? Is there a logic of salience-making analogous to that of belief?

We face here a problem with thoroughness. In speaking of belief, we found that we had to replace *B*-thoroughness with the more limited *B,E*-thoroughness. *S*-thoroughness calls for the same limitation for the same reason (to avoid a glut of directives). So let us try *S,E*-thoroughness: if *y* follows from the conjunction of all you make salient *and* you entertain *y*, you must make *y* salient.

This won't entirely do. A principle we have been taking for granted is that of *S,B-univocity*, that if you believe that *x* and *y* are coreportive and you make *x* salient, you can't also make *y* salient.[34] Suppose you believe that $p \cdot q$ and q are coreportive. (Let *q* be *Jack kissed Jill*; let *p* be *He kissed her on the cheek*.) Suppose you entertain *q*. Then, by *S,E*-thoroughness, if you make $p \cdot q$ salient, you must also make *q* salient, which would violate *S,B*-univocity. So we must qualify further. We must move to *S,E,B*-thoroughness: if *x* is the conjunction of all you make salient and y follows from x, and you entertain y, *and* you don't believe that y is coreportive with x or any conjunct of it, you must make y salient. I am willing to accept the judgments imposed by this principle along with our others.

No problem with *S*-consistency: if you make x salient, you can't make $\sim x$ salient. This follows directly from *B*-consistency. A person's making p salient is his selecting it from the propositions he believes about what p reports. A proposition that you make salient must thus be one you believe. By *B*-consistency, you can't believe both p and $\sim p$. So you can't make both salient either.

There is also *S*-reflection: you cannot make a proposition salient that would have to be false if you did (and were *S*-disciplined, i.e., *S, E, B*-thorough and *S*-consistent). You cannot make a proposition salient that you can't *properly* make salient. This doesn't follow from *B*-reflection, nor from that plus anything else. Still, I am willing to accept the judgments imposed by *S*-reflection along with the rest, e.g., that we can't make $p \cdot \sim Sp$ salient, or $p \cdot S\sim p$, etc.

My willingness to accept these judgments endorses the principles imposing them on me. Thus I have a logic of salience (or seeings) like that of belief alone – a set of principles for salience alone. And the propositions we can't properly make salient correspond to those we can't properly believe: they are the same with *S* in place of *B*. But the plural-attitude principles will very likely be of more interest, for these involve a modification of the usual logic of thought – in particular, of the usual principles of thoroughness and expectedness. If you believe x and you want y, and if z follows from $x \cdot y$, and neither x nor . . . , must you also want z? If you believe that y reports the outcome of what is reported by x and you want y, must you also want x? The usual answer is *yes* in both cases. On the logic here proposed, the answer both times is *not always*. Whether you must want z and x depends on your seeings, on what you make salient (recall *D, B, S*-thoroughness and *D, B, S*-expectedness).

What allows for this seeings-dependence is the rejection of extensionality, an idea designed to ensure that nothing depends on how things are seen. This brings up the second issue that we left open above. How can values that aren't extensional provide us with guidance for choice and for action? Doesn't our setting different values on propositions we think coreportive stick us too often with reasons for taking and also *not* taking the same action? Doesn't it lead us too often to having to toss a coin to decide?

Recall the gift/bribe case. Let g be *I take this gift*. Let b be *I take this bribe*. You think g and b coreportive, but you reject extensionality and want g though you don't want b. You also think $\sim g$ and $\sim b$ coreportive and want $\sim b$ though you don't want $\sim g$. And you believe that taking the money would make g true and that *not* taking it would make $\sim b$ true. Do you have reasons both for taking and for not taking the money?

Only if you make salient *In taking the money, I would g* and also make salient *In not taking it, I would* $\sim b$. Call these propositions α and β. Can you make both of them salient? I suggest that you can't – not if you are *S*-disciplined. I hold that *S*-discipline calls for a certain congruence of seeings in each issue, certain formally related propositions having to be either both salient or both not. If you think in certain terms when you consider doing a, you must also think in those terms when you consider *not* doing it.

More precisely, I accept this principle of *S,B*-congruence, that if you make salient *In x'ing, I would y* and believe *In* $\sim$*x'ing, I would* $\sim$*y*, you must also make salient *In* $\sim$*x'ing, I would* $\sim$*y*. In the gift/bribe case, if you make salient α: *In taking the money, I would g*, you must (by congruence) make salient δ: *In not taking the money, I would* $\sim g$. Since you think $\sim g$ and $\sim b$ coreportive, you think δ coreportive with β: *In not taking the money, I would* $\sim b$, and it follows (by *S,B*-univocity) that you can't make both δ and β salient. Thus if you make α salient, you can't make β salient, and you therefore (if you are disciplined) can't have a reason for taking the money and also for not taking it. (This still sometimes lets you have reasons both for doing and for not doing x, say where x and $\sim x$ are your only options, their U^+-utilities are exactly the same, and you see them each as having the maximal U^+-utility in the case. But such special cases are what coins are for.)

Some readers turn the tables. I have rejected extensionality because I hold that seeings matter. They accept extensionality and so they argue that seeings *don't* matter, that we don't need the S-principles, that the S-clauses in others can be dropped, that the resulting, simpler principles (plus extensionality) are all that we need. If they accept those principles, they must be willing to follow through, to make the judgments those simpler principles (plus extensionality) impose. They must be willing to say that Orwell, who wanted to shoot the fascist, should have wanted to shoot that "fellow creature" – that his *not* wanting it was a logical lapse. Also that, in the gift/bribe case, if you want to take the gift, you must want to take the bribe – that you are logically wrong if you don't. Also that, in the case described, if you want to be rich, you must want to kill your uncle – and are wrong if you don't. Holding that people's seeings don't matter calls for countless such judgments. If the critics accept these judgments, we are far apart. Their equilibria differ from mine, and perhaps I oughtn't to say that mine is better, that my logic is sounder.

Still, this may be too coy. Are all logics, all equilibria equal? I incline to say *no*. Sometimes we adjust our principles and judgments to more than each other (and to our beliefs). We adjust the whole package sometimes also to certain exogenous principles. And those outside, nonlogical matters sometimes then are decisive. They determine which of the equilibria we might establish we call the best. Here is one such external principle: avoid, if you can, all sweeping censure of the thinking other people do. If you find a possible alternative to faulting Orwell and others like him, opt for that alternative. (What makes an alternative *possible* for us? Its fitting into a reflective equilibrium we are willing to enter.)

I accept this last principle. It isn't a logical principle. It calls for looking to other people, to the judgments some *of them* make – it calls for being slow to fault them. In attending in that way to others, it is a principle of ethics, or at least of community, and it suggests that endorsing a logic takes us outside ourselves, outside mere inner cohesion. That provides for a broader basis of reflection on our logic. And it lets me consider my logic sounder than the usual sort, though sounder not on logical but on ethical grounds.

7

THE MEANING OF LIFE

NEAR the middle of Tolstoy's *Anna Karenina,* Levin is sitting in his bedroom listening to the sounds of his dying brother.

> [Levin's] thoughts were of the most various, but the end of all his thoughts was the same – death. Death, the inevitable end of all. . . . It was in himself too he felt [it]. If not today, tomorrow, if not tomorrow, in thirty years, wasn't it all the same! . . . He sat on his bed in the darkness, crouched up, hugging his knees, and holding his breath from the strain of thought, he pondered. But the more intensely he thought, the clearer it became to him that it was indubitably so, that in reality, looking upon life, he had forgotten one little fact – that death will come, and all ends, that nothing was even worth beginning.[1]

The thought of death and the void that follows sent Levin into despair. He remained as active as before, for the thought didn't always intrude, but "darkness had fallen upon everything for him." He even married and had a child, but at the core of all he did there was a sense of the pointlessness of it. "He saw nothing but death or the advance towards death in everything."[2]

Here is a report of the same awakening and of same reaction to it, this one from longer ago.

> The wise man's eyes are in his head; but the fool walketh in darkness: and I myself perceived also that one event happeneth to them all. Then said I in my heart, as it happeneth to the fool, so it happeneth even to me; and why was I then

> more wise? ... [T]here is no remembrance of the wise more than of the fool for ever; seeing that which now is in the days to come shall all be forgotten.... Therefore I hated life ... for all is vanity and vexation of spirit.[3]

Levin said later that his life had no meaning, and the Preacher for whom all was vanity might have said that too. Countless people, before and after, have found themselves thinking the same.

Philosophers sometimes comment on this, mostly from the sidelines, speaking to the Levins of the world, trying to help them to cope. Usually they try to lead them back into the light of day, sometimes even to show them where their thinking went wrong. I will not be trying that. Levin's thinking deserves respect, even from those who don't share it. Levin, the Preacher, and those who think like them are thinking as sensible people do. Still, those who reject their despairing conclusion are thinking sensibly too (and that includes Levin at the end of the book). This is not a paradox, but wrapping our minds around the idea calls for some analysis.

1

My basic question is modest. It doesn't ask whether life has a meaning and, if so, what that meaning is. It is not about life in general but about particular lives, and about how lives are judged by the people whose lives they are. It asks only what Levin reported when he said that his life lacked meaning, that it had no meaning *for him* – and what all those others report who say the same about theirs.

Let me first propose this, that such a report is a summary judgment, a summary of many particular judgments about particular actions or projects. The judgments are that *this* one doesn't matter, and *that* one doesn't matter either, and this third matters just as little, ... that in fact none of them matter – that "nothing [is] even worth beginning." Our life being all that we do, if none of our doings matter to us, our life has no meaning for us. So the question reduces to this: what is a person saying when he says that doing *x* doesn't matter, that it doesn't matter *to him* whether or not he does it?

Here is the core idea. Say that a person asks himself what his doing *x* would lead to, what would later be true if he did it. He thinks of the likely total sequel or outcome of his doing *x*, and he lets his assessment of that be his assessment of doing *x*[4]. In a common formulation, the utility he sets on doing *x* is the utility of its expected outcome. The utility for him of *not* doing *x* is the utility of the outcome of *that*. If doing *x* and not doing *x* are very close in utility for him (relative to his utility scale, to the difference between its top and bottom),[5] it doesn't matter to this person whether or not he does it.[6] His doing *x* itself doesn't matter. And, again, if this is true of every *x* for this person – if nothing he did would matter to him – then life has no meaning for him.

Note that the utilities need just be close; they need not be the same. Even a person in despair keeps himself from stepping into puddles. Stepping and *not* stepping in them aren't the same in utility, but the difference is very small (relative to any utility scale). Not too small to affect what we do: everyone avoids a puddle. But too small to give a life meaning. Staying dry can't cancel despair.

Now to Levin and the Preacher and the others like them. Looking to what would follow for them if they did this or that, they all see death at the end. Death is not all they see; much may happen before that. The total outcome of doing *x* is a conjunction of many events, and the value of doing *x* is the value of that conjunction. Still, whenever they think about it, the prospect of death spills over the rest – the *horror* of it spills over. Every total outcome-prospect is then steeped in horror. For Levin, the "little fact" of death merged with all that might yet precede it, and the value he set on each prospect came to be that which he set on death. In his reflections on what he might do, his life was swallowed up by death.[7]

In a letter, Tolstoy writes, "Once a man has realized that death is the end of everything, there is nothing worse than life either."[8] That is hardly true for all, but it was true for Levin. He made sure that his fields were sown, he pensioned his aged peasants, he supported his sister-in-law. He knew he had to do these things, but doing them gave him no satisfaction, for in the light of his hard "little fact," doing and *not* doing them came to the same – they came to the same utility-wise. (Better, again: to so close to the same that the differences didn't count.) Nothing whatever thus mattered to him, and his life had no meaning for him.

This speaks of the effect on certain people of the death that awaits them. There are sometimes other events the awareness of which has the same effect. Some of these may be in the past.[9] Where a spouse or a child has died, a despair of the same sort may follow. In such cases, the horror of it shadows every action we take; in these cases, *fore*shadows it. Here too, the judgment we make of each prospect folds into that of the horror, and nothing we do then matters.

Nor need a death be a part of it, neither our own nor others'. Think of divorce or a separation or of some other collapse of our hopes. No horror there, but we sometimes despair. Or we may once have acted so badly that what we did has now come to haunt us. It then doesn't matter to us what we now do or don't do, for, whatever would still follow, what back then we did would remain and would swamp all else.

Again, the basic idea is this: a person's life lacks meaning for him where no action matters to him, and no action matters to him where, whatever x he considers, the utilities he sets on doing x and *not* doing it are very close – perhaps because his valuations of the x-contexts are all-overriding. This, I think, is on the right track, but it has to be qualified.

Think of Romeo and Juliet. The poison hadn't worked, and they are living happily after, surrounded by ten beautiful children and their two reconciled families. Say that today they have to decide whether or not to do *x*: should they or should they not go on a picnic by the lake? They would have bliss whatever they do, and all the rest would merge with that bliss, so it may not matter to them, and neither would any other *x* matter. On the analysis suggested above, life has no meaning for them.

Bliss is certainly rare, but many people know moments of it, where what they do doesn't matter to them since they will do it with HIM or with HER. Should we say that, at such moments, life has no meaning for them? It would be foolish to say that here, for we want to make sense of a kind of despair people sometimes are in, and what is common to bliss and despair cannot help us with that. So we will have to qualify. Adding one clause will do it: no action matters to a person where, whatever *x* he considers, the utilities he sets on doing *x* and *not* doing it are very close, and his life lacks meaning for him where those utilities are very close *and very low*.[10]

In bliss, the utilities, for every *x*, of doing *x* and of not doing it are very close but aren't low, so it doesn't matter to the blissful what they do but their life retains meaning. There are sometimes other such cases that have nothing to do with bliss. The Preacher said that all was vanity not just because of the sureness of death. He spoke too of life's being unfair: "the race is not to the swift, nor the battle to the strong, . . . nor yet riches to men of understanding, nor yet favor to men of skill."[11] Also of its repeating itself, of its all having been seen before: "there is no new thing under the sun."[12] Where life is unfair or just an old story, the utilities of doing and of not doing *x* may be close *without* being low, in which case our life retains meaning. Unfairness makes for sadness or anger; lack of interest makes for ennui. Neither makes for despair.

Is all this too shallow? Some will say that it is, that the problem of meaning is deeper than the problem that Levin is facing.

Levin's problem is personal: how ought he to cope with his judgment that nothing he ever might do would matter? The deeper problem is not about Levin but about us all together. The problem is, how should we live? Are there directives for people to follow, directives people *always* must follow? If so, what are those directives?

A belief in universal directives often involves believing in God, and people who lose their belief in God lose their faith in directives too. They may feel the loss of that faith as their being cut adrift, which may then make for despair. But many today were never believers, and this despair doesn't touch them. Their personal, "shallower" problem of meaning – if and when they encounter it – doesn't torment them any the less. And even people who (like Levin) do believe in God's directives sometimes must cope with the "shallower" problem. To them, it then doesn't seem shallow.[13]

2

I said that Levin and the others thought as sensible people do. Reflecting on *x* and *y* and *z*, they looked to the total outcomes and formed their judgments of what was worth doing in the light of how they valued those outcomes. Their despairing conclusion accorded with expectedness logic. This doesn't mean that sensible people who know that some day they will die must despair. The thinking of those who don't despair may accord with that logic too. Here are two such ways of thinking – call them the Localist and the Christian. Neither sort of thinking moves me, so I will be brief.

The localist says that he keeps to the present. He devalues all future events because of their being in the future, and the more distant an event is, the more he now devalues it. The further off it is, the lower its present value to him – the lower its *time-discounted* value. "In time the world will cool and everything will die; but that is a long time off still, and its present value at compound interest is almost nothing."[14] Suppose he thinks his own death far off. He then doesn't, as Levin did, assign it now some consuming disvalue. Its time-discounted disvalue for him may be "almost nothing," and the prospect of his dying may now leave him unconcerned. (Correspondingly for events in the past, for traumas or losses and the like; he discounts their disvalue too.)

Often, of course, discounting makes sense. Say we are thinking of buying an annuity. Say that the payout will only begin when we get to be 80. How likely are we to reach that age? It makes good sense to discount payouts by the improbability of getting them. But we can't apply that to death: we are sure to live long enough to die. Besides, the localist isn't discounting what may happen by its improbability but by its mere distance from him. Should time-distance be given such weight? Should it where we are thinking of death? You don't discount (devalue) your death by how many miles from here you will die. Why then should you discount it by how many *years* away that will be? Levin put it this way: "If not today, tomorrow, if not tomorrow, in thirty years, [isn't] it all the same!"

The second kind of thinking is more common. Newspapers refer obliquely to it in their reports of disasters: "Parents of victims asking *why*," "Mourners searching for reasons." The mourners are looking for solace, for what might soften their grief. Some may even want to hear that it all was part of a plan, that death is not really an end. They then want Christian assurance: "All his might Death must forgo, for now he's nought but idle show. His sting is lost forever. . . . For Death is swallowed up by Life, and all his power is ended."[15]

I said that a person aware of his death as the end of all he does may find the horror of that death trumping whatever preceded it. His life is then swallowed up by death. The Christian believes there is more to come and that its special glory trumps death – that "death is swallowed up by life," by the life that comes after. A person who believes this cannot despair; for him, every total prospect is bright.[16] Levin didn't believe it, and he would never have come to believe it. So I will drop this line too.

No doubt the most common response to despair is today the pharmacologist's. This offers not a new way of thinking but a new way of detaching from thought, from the judgment that leads to despair. It involves taking Prozac or Zoloft or some other drug like it.

A few words here will suffice.[17] Our judgments of meaning, our valuations, aren't defined by how we *feel*. Still, for most people, there is a connection. A person aware that all his prospects are bad, that his life is hopeless for him, very often is in despair. He *feels* the hopelessness of it. Prozac may get him around that. Though his life remain what it was, he may, taking Prozac, no longer *feel* bad, which may then sometimes get him to act so as to make his life better. The drug is thus a cure for despair but not a cure for what caused it (except, again, sometimes indirectly). For many people, that is good enough, and I can't say they are wrong. Still, Levin wouldn't have taken the drug. He wanted meaning, not mood enhancement. So I won't speak of this either.

3

The localist's advice to Levin is to revalue what hasn't yet happened, all that is still in the future. The Christian advice is to revise his beliefs, to believe in an afterlife. Both these ways of avoiding despair comport with the mainstream logic of thought, in which a person's beliefs and values are the basic independent factors. Tolstoy offers a different approach, and in the end Levin seizes on it. The case he lays out is far from persuasive; most of his readers are not persuaded. But the logic it rests on is sound, and so we have to consider it.

Both in *War and Peace* and in *Anna Karenina,* Tolstoy is pressing a metaphysics. In *War and Peace,* he spells it out at great (and sometimes tedious) length. In *Anna Karenina,* it isn't mentioned, but both the story of Anna's life and that of Levin's illustrate it. Its basic point is that thinking and planning have no real lasting importance, that all that happens (except on the margin) is fully determined by mindless events, by countless minute antecedents.[18] The natural laws that govern what happens are unknown and unknowable; they involve the "integration" of the unthinking minutiae. People who claim to know them are foolish, and those who try to act on their foolishness only make trouble for others.

No one knows the laws of nature, but those who don't even try to know them sometimes sense their drift; they sense what the laws make possible and what the laws exclude. They also sense what *has to* happen. They don't pretend to know the details, but they intuit the flow of things. This intuition of nature is *wisdom*. Tolstoy speaks of ignorant peasants as often much wiser than their masters, though those of their masters who don't claim knowledge sometimes have wisdom too.[19] In *War and Peace*, both the conscript Karataev and the Commander-in-Chief, Kutuzov, had it.

In *Anna Karenina*, Levin had it. Near the end of the novel,

> When Levin thought what he was and what he was living for, he could find no answer to [his] questions and was reduced to despair, but he left off questioning himself . . . [and] acted and lived resolutely and without hesitation. . . . [T]hough he experienced no delight at all at the thought of the work he was doing, he felt a complete conviction of its necessity. . . . To live the same family life as his father and forefathers – that is, in the same condition of culture – and to bring up his children in the same, was incontestably necessary. It was as necessary as dining when one was hungry. And to do this, just as it was necessary to cook dinner, it was necessary to keep the mechanism of agriculture at [his estate] going so as to yield an income, . . . to look after the land himself, not to lease it, and to breed cattle, to manure the fields, and plant timber.[20]

Tolstoy notes that "all this . . . filled up the whole of Levin's life, which had no meaning at all for him when he began to think."[21] The last clause carries the message. The problem that plagued him came up for Levin only "at the thought of" his life, only "when [he] thought what he was and what he was living for." At other times, he lived his life both vigorously and well. Tolstoy asks, "What did this mean? It meant that he had been living rightly but thinking wrongly."[22]

This leads him to ask how Levin must change in order to think rightly. He answers that Levin had to come to see what he did in the light of his wisdom (in Tolstoy's special sense of that), that he had to come to see what he did as what nature required. Levin *knew* he was doing what, in his shoes, he had to do, that it all needed doing – that it was "incontestably necessary." He knew that he was playing the part that nature had prepared for him. Still, he didn't report his doings to himself that way. He didn't *grasp* or *see* them so.

Often he saw them in no way at all ("he left off questioning himself"). Tolstoy says that he wasn't then thinking. At other times, he saw them as doing this or that *while moving toward death*, and then, Tolstoy holds, he was thinking wrongly. Nature called for his sowing and reaping, his planting timber and cutting it down and, in time, for his dying too. He needed not only to *know* that but also to *see* all he did in that light. Levin came to agree. He came to see every possible action as going with or against the flow, with or against the drift of all nature. And that perspective shook off despair.

Levin's conversion is the climax of the book, but I will pass that by. It is not compelling. A peasant spoke of another peasant as "living for his soul," as "not forgetting God," and Levin went "breathless with excitement."[23] This isn't likely to be of much use to others in Levin's shoes. (It didn't provide for Tolstoy himself when he faced his own despair, a despair that was very like Levin's.)[24] Better also not to consider whether one always ought to see things in terms of their going with the flow. Seeing implies believing: you can't see something in *this* way or *that* unless you believe it *is* that way. Tolstoy's idea of the right way of seeing implies his conviction that there *is* a flow. It implies his metaphysics, and it won't pay to get into that.

I want to raise a different question. Though Levin still knew he was going to die, that no longer was a part of how he saw his life. As a result, his life regained meaning, and the despair that had plagued him lifted. How could that have happened? I say that someone's life lacks meaning where, whatever *x* he considers, the utilities he sets on doing *x* and *not* doing it are very close and very low. This speaks only of the utilities set on doing and *not* doing *x*, and Levin's conversion changed no utilities he set. He set the same, before and after, on moving toward death by doing *x* and also the same, before and after, on moving toward death by *not* doing *x*. And he set the same utilities, before and after, on keeping to nature by doing *x* and the same too, before and after, on going against it by *not* doing *x*. His conversion changing no utilities, how could it make things matter to him that hadn't mattered before?

This puzzle comes of cutting corners. I have spoken of setting utilities on this or that action or outcome-situation, but a sounder analysis here speaks not of actions but of *propositions*. What we set some utility on is then not action *x* or *y* but the proposition that *We do x* or that *We will do y* or that *This or that will happen*. Any action can be reported or propositionalized differently, and different utilities may be set on different propositions reporting the same, even where we know they report the same action or same situation. Still, at any single time, only one (often compound) proposition expresses the way we see things, and the utilities that enter our judgment of whether our life has meaning for us are those that we set on the propositions expressing *how we see* this or that. This means that the utilities a person sets aren't the only relevant factors. How he sees what is involved is always relevant too, for that determines which of the utilities that he now sets now count for him, which of them bear on the issue before him.[25]

What I should have said is this: that nothing matters to a person where, whatever *x* he considers, the utilities he sets on the propositions expressing *how he sees* his doing *x* and *not* doing *x* are very close, and that his life lacks meaning for him where those utilities are very low. Before his conversion, Levin saw all he might do in terms of his moving toward death. Afterwards, he saw it all in terms of his going with the flow. The propositions that figured then for him were not *In planting* (or *not planting*) *an orchard, I would be moving toward death* but *In planting* (or *not planting*) *it, I would* (or *wouldn't*) *be following nature*. The utilities he set remained what they were, but the utilities that counted for him when he asked himself "what he lived for" were those he set on these latter propositions, on the ones that were salient for him after his conversion; and these utilities were different from those he set on the coreportive pre-conversion ones. (And they were neither low nor close.)

What gave his post-conversion life meaning wasn't any new values he had, any new utility settings. Nor was it some discovery, a new belief he had come to – "I have discovered nothing. I have only found out what I knew."[26] Rather, it was his new way of seeing, a new perspective on things. Tolstoy's message (minus the metaphysics) is that meaning isn't discovered, that it is *imposed* on life, and that we impose it on our own lives – or fail to do that – by how we see what we do.

4

This point is applied to Levin-sort problems by writers whose thinking is very different from Tolstoy's. Here is the Stoic Epictetus:

> We must make the best of those things that are in our power, and take the rest as nature gives it. . . . I must die. But must I die groaning? I must be imprisoned. But must I whine as well?

> I must suffer exile. Can anyone then hinder me from going with a smile, and a good courage, and at peace? . . .
>
> For since you must die in any case, you must be found doing something – whatever it be – farming or digging or trading or holding the consulship or suffering indigestion or diarrhea. What then would you have death find you doing? For my part, I would be found busy with some humane task. . . . If death finds me thus occupied, I am content.[27]

This isn't a sour-grapes policy: if what you want isn't in your power, get yourself to stop wanting it. It doesn't say, since you can't avoid death, get yourself to stop caring. It says, don't dwell on what can't be avoided. Look only at what is in your power, never at what is not. Don't let yourself think of the future in terms of all you know will happen, for some of that is *bound* to happen. Ignore what is bound to happen! What you do will then matter to you, and your life will have meaning for you.

Another way of putting this, still about how we should see things: think of what you might now do in terms of the difference it would make, in terms of how your doing it would improve (or worsen) things. See it in the light of how what would follow would differ from the outcome of your staying in bed. This calls for your not seeing your actions in terms of the death that awaits you or in terms of what you did or suffered in the past. It calls for your seeing them only in terms of what they would causally bring about.

The Preacher has yet another ideology, this one more like the Epicurean:

> Go thy way, eat thy bread with joy, and drink thy wine with a merry heart. . . . Let thy garments be always white, and let thy head lack no ointment. Live joyfully with the wife whom thou lovest all the days of the life of thy vanity. . . . Whatsoever thy hand findest to do, do it with thy might; for there is no work, nor device, nor knowledge, nor wisdom, in the grave, whither thou goest.[28]

The Preacher is saying, find small pleasures. Your bread, your wine, and your love are before you and can be enjoyed though all remains vanity. They can be enjoyed if you look to the short run, if you ignore the rest. To those who see every situation against the background of all they know, nothing is ever worth doing. To you, if you screen off all but the moment, what you do will matter. The life you lead will have meaning. It will have the meaning it has because you will have imposed it, and you will have imposed that meaning by blocking from view the vanity of it.[29]

5

How we think can torment us. It can also relieve us. Here is Jack, complaining to Jill, "My son is a disaster; my daughter is worse. The rest of the family isn't talking to me. I am about to lose my job. All my friends are sleazeballs," etc. Jill's advice is, "Be philosophical – don't think about it!" She isn't advising Jack on what to attend to in his mess of a life, only on what to *ignore*. The Preacher did much the same, and so did Epictetus; they said, "Ignore the Big Picture!" Tolstoy put it differently, telling his readers to *see things this way* ("Always look to what nature demands!"), but that implied *don't see them as you did*, and so he too urged selective ignorings. Can it be right to advise a person to shake off his troubles by ignoring them? Does that not counsel self-deception? Did Levin come to deceive himself?

A self-deceiver gets himself to reject a painful belief. He gets himself to believe something he now believes is false because he would be happier if he believed it true. Say that Jack convinced himself that his family loved him, that he was going to get a promotion, that his friends were heroes and saints; this would be self-deception. Levin never came to think that he wouldn't die, and the Preacher never concluded that life *wasn't* vanity. Neither ever stopped believing anything he believed before. So they didn't deceive themselves. They changed the way they were seeing things – they changed the perspectives they took – but their beliefs remained what they were.

They rejected a painful perspective in favor of one they could live with; why is that not a self-deception? A change of perspective is a revision, a re-*vision* of things, and a vision can't be deceptive. This because deception has to bring in some falsehood or other, and a seeing can't falsify. A seeing selects from what we think is true. It is an attending-to-*this* and not *that*. No change in how we see things alone can fix on a falsehood where there was none before. If my life is half over, I can't be wrong to see it that way; nor can I be wrong to see it as *I have half my life left*. And if I see my situation as *I have half my life left* when I don't, it isn't my view of my situation that is false but my underlying belief.

A seeing can't be false, and neither can it be true; neither "true" nor "false" applies. What then is the point of urging this or that view on us? What are Tolstoy and the others doing? They are doing philosophy, though not the sort most philosophers do. They offer no analyses – only reminders and exhortations. Their writings are meant to help a person find his way out of some maze he is in, out of some inner turmoil, to help the fly out of the fly-bottle.[30]

There is no true or false of that bottle, only an in and an out. So a person brought out of his bottle can't be being deceived, and neither can he deceive himself where he brings himself out. Still, a gnawing question remains. Can't there sometimes be a self-*blinding* in his ceasing to see what he saw? Can't he sometimes be keeping himself from seeing what he ought to be seeing? What did Tolstoy mean when he said that Levin was thinking "wrongly"? He didn't mean that his views were in error but that their focus was off, that they distorted the way things were. Certain *changes* of seeings likewise counted for Tolstoy as being wrong – as being not false but distortive. But what sense can be made of the concept of grasping the truth in a way that distorts it?

Here is a gruesome case.[31] Franz Grassler, a former Nazi commissioner of the Warsaw ghetto, is speaking to Claude Lanzmann in the documentary *Shoah*. Grassler describes his official activities as "maintaining the ghetto." Lanzmann objects to the phrase. Five thousand people died every month – one cannot speak there of "maintenance." Grassler insists on the way that he put it. "But people were dying in the streets. There were bodies everywhere," says Lanzmann. "That was the paradox," Grassler replies.[32] When Lanzmann says that the ghetto served only to set up those in it for being killed, Grassler concedes that fact. Yet he firmly holds to the view that he was then "maintaining the ghetto."

One can guess why he stuck to this. It is likely he saw very early that the ghetto was just a holding pen, that he had got involved in the management of a killing operation. It may be too that at some point or other he became uneasy with this, perhaps (perhaps!) even agonized by it. Getting himself to see what he did as "maintaining the ghetto" let him avoid the horror. Nothing he did could have mattered to him had he remained, in his own eyes, a killer.

Grassler's change was no self-deception. He had in fact been maintaining that ghetto: he kept those in it from getting away. Still, if he came to see what he did as an involvement in a slaughter and was then horrified by it, may we not fault the easy re-vision that threw off that horror? May we not call it a misconstrual, a willful distortion of the truth? Yes, but what is a proper construal and what is a misconstrual – what *makes* it a misconstrual?

No need to dwell on Grassler here. The basic issue is not one of evil and of painting it over. It is an issue of everyday life. Are we seeing this or that right? *Is* there a right way of seeing it, a way that is somehow *objectively* right? Can we see all we do as we please, or are some seeings – or changes of seeings – misconstruals and sometimes self-blindings? These questions are dark, but they can't be avoided.

NOTES

ESSAY 1

1. In my *Understanding Action*, Cambridge: Cambridge University Press, 1991, p. 1ff and passim.
2. George Orwell, "Looking Back on the Spanish Civil War," in his *A Collection of Essays*, Garden City: Doubleday, 1957, p. 199.
3. I report the actual case in my "Allowing for Understandings," *Journal of Philosophy* 89 (1992). Other cases like it are discussed in Essay 3.
4. I say more in *Understanding Action* and in my *Making Choices*, Cambridge: Cambridge University Press, 1997, and in Essay 4.
5. This isn't the usual concept of ambiguity; that applies only to words and sentences (such as "She lost her interest when she lost her money").
6. Again, not the usual concept of meaning having to do with sentences.
7. This issue was first raised in Peter Diamond, "Cardinal Welfare, Individualistic Ethics, and Interpersonal Comparison of Utilities: A Comment," *Journal of Political Economy* 75 (1967).
8. Leo Tolstoy, *War and Peace*, Harmondsworth: Penguin, 1982, p. 1242.
9. Not so, of course, vice versa; recall *I kill that fascist* (p) and *I kill that fellow creature* (q).
10. There remain many problems here; see Colin McGinn, *Mental Content*, Oxford: Basil Blackwell, 1989. I say more about propositions in my *Understanding Action*, pp. 71–8.
11. This cuts corners, for seeing implies believing, and we don't know which outcomes will hold – don't now *believe* that *this* or *that* will. For a fuller analysis, see Essay 6 (the final expectedness principles).
12. This first appeared in print (attributed to Richard Zeckhauser) in Daniel Kahneman and Amos Tversky, "Prospect Theory: An

Analysis of Decision Under Risk," *Econometrica* 47 (1979), p. 283.

13. If you hold that, since your life is at stake, you would pay all you have in both cases, say you will have to shoot yourself not in the head but the toe.
14. From its having been presented in Maurice Allais, "Le Comportement de l'homme rationnel devant le risque: Critique des postulats et axiomes de l'école américaine," *Econometrica* 21 (1953).
15. A formally similar analysis (noting the irrelevance of columns 1 through 5) can be offered of the Zeckhauser problem.
16. Again, "/*w*" is counterfactual; it isn't short for "and I will regret it."
17. I put this differently in Essay 6 (see note 11 above). In my *Understanding Action* and my "Attending to Understandings," I offer a more elaborate concept I now think isn't needed. My line in "Rationality: A Third Dimension," *Economics and Philosophy* 3 (1987), got nowhere.
18. John Broome, *Weighing Goods,* Oxford: Basil Blackwell, 1991, Chapter 5. Broome says that outcomes are different "if and only if they differ in a way that makes it rational to have a preference between them" (p. 103). But this comes to the way I put it if we suppose (as I do) that preferences hold only between propositions and that any difference between propositions allows for someone to have a rational preference between them.
19. This follows Donald Davidson, "The Individuation of Events, " in his *Essays on Actions and Events,* Oxford: Oxford University Press, 1980.
20. This wasn't always so in the past. See my *Understanding Action,* Chapter 3 – in particular, the section on Aristotle, pp. 55–60.
21. See Howard Raiffa, *Decision Analysis,* Reading, MA: Addison-Wesley, 1968; Richard Jeffrey, "Risk and Human Rationality," *Monist* 70 (1987); and John Broome, "Uncertainty and Fairness," *Economic Journal* 94 (1994) and his *Weighing Goods*. A related line is taken in Philip Pettit, "Decision Theory and Folk Psychology," in Michael Bacharach and Susan Hurley (eds.), *Essays in the Foundations of Decision Theory,* Oxford: Basil Blackwell, 1991.
22. Amos Tversky, "A Critique of Expected Utility Theory: Descriptive and Normative Considerations," *Erkenntnis* 9 (1975), p. 171.
23. Mark Machina, "Dynamic Consistency and Non-Expected Utility Models," *Journal of Economic Literature* 27 (1989), p. 1662.
24. Brian Skyrms, review of my *Making Choices, TLS (Times Literary Supplement),* Feb. 6, 1998, p. 30.

25. Ibid.
26. For more on the total-belief principle, see Essay 4.
27. I speak of extensionality in Essays 4 and 6.
28. I take up these questions in Essay 6.

ESSAY 2

1. Jack's partition might there be: *Either all the others will do as I will, or all but one will do as I will (that one doing the opposite), or all but two will do as I will....*
2. This is noted in Isaac Levi, "Prediction, Deliberation, and Correlated Equilibria" in Levi's *The Covenant of Reason*, Cambridge: Cambridge University Press, 1997, pp. 102–3.
3. See John Maynard Smith, *Evolution and the Theory of Games*, Cambridge: Cambridge University Press, 1982, pp. 161ff. Also Robert Axelrod, *The Evolution of Cooperation*, New York: Basic Books, 1984, Chapter 5 (written with William D. Hamilton).
4. The two-by-four matrix whose columns are headed *A, O, S*-regardless, and *T*-regardless – in the response-option reading of these – is the matrix of Nigel Howard's 2-metagame of the Prisoners' Dilemma (in his *Paradoxes of Rationality*, Cambridge, MA: MIT Press, 1971). I discuss Howard's metagame theory in my "Cooperation and Contracts," *Economics and Philosophy* 8 (1992).
5. The contrast here is not between uncertainty and certainty but between uncertainty and risk.
6. Better, not *every* constriction; only those that generate points meeting certain conditions – for instance, that the sum of the (point) probabilities of x and of $\sim x$ is 1. The interconnection of probabilistic and utility-uncertainty also complicates things, but we are speaking of probabilities only.
7. I develop this idea in my *Having Reasons*, Princeton: Princeton University Press, 1984, especially pp. 23–4 and 43–5. A closely related analysis appears in Isaac Levi, "On Indeterminate Probabilities," *Journal of Philosophy* 71 (1974), and in his *The Enterprise of Knowledge*, Cambridge, MA: MIT Press, 1980, Chapter 4.
8. Independence under risk is the special instance of this in which the ranges are zero.
9. The only exception is that in which the assignments are the same to all four entries.
10. Where the dominance is the simple dominance of a Prisoners' Dilemma. A matrix revealing *super*dominance is immune to such

transformations. (An option is superdominant in a matrix if each of its possible outcomes is preferred to *every* outcome of every other.)

11. Paul Samuelson, the economist, goes further. He writes somewhere that maximining isn't a principle of rationality but of paranoia.
12. For the details, see Nelson Goodman, "A Query on Confirmation," *Journal of Philosophy* 43 (1946) and his *Fact, Fiction, and Forecast*, 4th ed., Cambridge, MA: Harvard University Press, 1983, Chapter 3.
13. Goodman's own line is different; see his *Fact, Fiction, and Forecast*, Chapter 4. For some discussion of Goodman, see Douglas Stalker (ed.), *Grue! The New Riddle of Induction*, Chicago: Open Court, 1994.
14. Goodman rejects the idea; see his *Fact, Fiction and Forecast*, Chapter 3. Say that you are Jack; what more must you do than listen to Jill to learn whether she is doing the same as you?
15. We might put the situation more abstractly still, as a Prisoners' *Predicament*, by dropping the independence condition. That would provide for P-Predicaments that are not P-Plights, and so for the possibility noted in the last paragraph of Section 1.
16. Again, they may be in Figure 2.3 and in neither 2.1 nor 2.2, for it may be that one or the other hasn't yet partitioned.
17. John von Neumann and Oskar Morgenstern, *Theory of Games and Economic Behavior*, 3rd ed., New York: Wiley, 1964, p. 12.
18. Actions being *the same* or *the opposite* only under given descriptions, an admonition has to make clear *how* we should think of other people acting as we do or the opposite way.
19. See Gerald Marwell and Ruth E. Ames, "Economists Free Ride, Does Anyone Else?: Experiments on the Provision of Public Goods, IV," *Journal of Public Economics* 15 (1981). The authors remark that "Economics graduate students . . . were much more likely to free ride than any of our other groups of subjects" (pp. 306–7). They suggest that "Economists . . . may start behaving according to the general tenets of the theories they study" (p. 309), though they note there also may be some preselection of those who enter the field.

ESSAY 3

1. Richard H. Thaler, "Toward a Positive Theory of Consumer Choice," *Journal of Economic Behavior and Organization* 1 (1980),

reprinted in Thaler's *Quasi Rational Economics*, New York: Russell Sage Foundation, 1991, p. 8.

2. Daniel Kahneman, Jack L. Knetsch, and Richard H. Thaler, "Experimental Tests of the Endowment Effect and the Coase Theorem," *Journal of Political Economy* 98 (1990), reprinted in Thaler's *Quasi Rational Economics*, p. 169.
3. Amos Tversky and Daniel Kahneman, "Loss Aversion in Riskless Choice: A Reference-Dependent Model," *Quarterly Journal of Economics* 106 (1991), p. 1041.
4. Thaler, "Toward a Positive Theory . . . ," p. 7.
5. Thaler, *Quasi Rational Economics*, pp. xi–xii.
6. William Samuelson and Richard Zeckhauser, "Status Quo Bias in Decision Making," *Journal of Risk and Uncertainty* 1 (1988).
7. Daniel Kahneman and Amos Tversky, "Prospect Theory: An Analysis of Decision Under Risk," *Econometrica* 47 (1979), and "Choices, Values and Frames," *American Psychologist* 39 (1984).
8. Hence the need in Thaler's study for "if the risk were greater by .001 than in fact it was." (There the good at issue was *safety*.)
9. "Loss Aversion in Riskless Choice . . . ," p. 1041.
10. The value/disvalue of x is measured here in terms of the second good y; putting aside some difficulties, we might let that be money.
11. This assumes that the shape of a two-goods indifference curve is like that of a one-good gain/loss value curve. There are experimental studies that confirm this likeness; e.g., Jack L. Knetsch, "Preference and Nonreversibility of Indifference Curves," *Journal of Economic Behavior and Organization* 17 (1992). (Knetsch shows a two-goods gain curve and loss curve intersecting [p. 135]. The gain curve below the intersection and the loss curve above it compose a two-goods indifference curve.)
12. More broadly put, the question is whether loss aversion makes for $\mathrm{WTA}_\beta(y, x_\beta, x_\alpha) > \mathrm{WTP}_\alpha(y, x_\beta, x_\alpha)$ for every status-quo point β and would-have-had point α such that x_β is the x-holding at β and x_α is that at α, $x_\beta > x_\alpha$. A still more comprehensive concept of endowment effects is that, for some positive $x' \leq (x_\beta - x_\alpha)$, $\mathrm{WTA}_{\beta,x'}(y, \beta, x') > \mathrm{WTP}_{\alpha,x'}(y, \alpha, x')$, where $\mathrm{WTA}_{\beta,x'}(y, \beta, x')$ is the least amount of y we would at β be willing to accept as compensation for losing x' and $\mathrm{WTP}_{\alpha,x'}(y, \alpha, x')$ is the most of y we would at α be willing to pay to gain x'.
13. The earlier principle of diminishing sensitivity compares our valuations of gains/losses of different sizes. This one compares valuations of same-sized gains/losses at different holdings of x.

14. This supposes that $y_2 - y_1$ is small. I am taking no stand on what happens when it isn't small.
15. None of the many experiments reported brings out such a case, but this is as it should be, for, in them all, $x_1 - x_2$ is small; e.g., in *b* there is only one more mug (or pen or the like) than in *a*.
16. Tversky and Kahneman hold to the contrary because they define loss aversion in terms of *two* basing points ("Loss Aversion in Riskless Choice . . . ," p. 1047). On their definition, loss aversion *is* the endowment effect.
17. Again, recall the qualification in note 14.
18. There is both a converse status-quo bias and a converse endowment effect here. If $I_{b'}$ passed closely *above a*, a converse endowment effect would remain but there would be neither sort of bias: *b′* would be preferred to *a* both at *b′* and at *a*.
19. In their "Loss Aversion in Riskless Choice. . . ."
20. Strictly, on Tversky and Kahneman's theory (as also on mine, see note 25), a person has many indifference$_a$ curves and many indifference$_b$ curves, etc. For every point *a* and every other point *r*, he has an I_a curve through *r*; *a* itself is on only one of these curves.
21. This goes beyond Tversky and Kahneman, who doubt that a general stand can be taken on the rationality of preference indexing and of status-quo bias; see their "Loss Aversion in Riskless Choice . . . ," pp. 1057–8.
22. Here *q* and *r* are different propositions describing the same situation (being at *c*), though their difference is of course such that they can't both be true.
23. I_b does not show the agent at *b* preferring *b to a* simpliciter. This is the modification promised in Section 2.
24. As on the usual economic analysis, two *havings* curves can't cross.
25. It may sometimes be useful to speak of g/l curves more inclusively, to say that, for every *a*, a person has a curve of that sort through each set of points such that he is indifferent at *a* regarding all moves from *a* to these points. (Only one of these curves goes through *a*, each has its point of inflection on the same vertical as *a*, and none of them can cross.)
26. In my *Making Choices*, Cambridge: Cambridge University Press, 1997; also in my *Understanding Action*, Cambridge: Cambridge University Press, 1991. Also in Essay 4.
27. At this last step, the argument assumes the interpersonal comparability of utility.

28. Here of course *y* can't be money. It has to be something not counting as wealth – perhaps days-yet-to-live.
29. Recall the "still more comprehensive" concept of endowment effects in note 12. Our analysis in Section 1 is here applied to that.
30. Where $x_1 - x_2$ is large, there may be *converse* endowment effects, and that would argue for equalization.
31. Ronald Dworkin, "What Is Equality? Part II: Equality of Resources," *Philosophy and Public Affairs* 10 (1981), p. 285.
32. The opposite may be true where some bundles differ greatly in size, this because there might then be some *converse* status-quo bias.
33. I say more on the rightness of seeings in Essay 4.
34. "Prospect Theory . . . ," p. 273.
35. That is, it isn't inconsistent unless we assume extensionality; for that, see Essays 4 and 6.
36. The numbers in Figure 3.4 refer to dollars, not utilities. Thus they aren't subject to a linear transformation that would cancel the minuses (losses).
37. Thaler, "The Psychology of Choice and the Assumptions of Economics," in Alvin Roth (ed.), *Laboratory Experiments in Economics*, Cambridge: Cambridge University Press, 1987, reprinted in Thaler's *Quasi Rational Economics*, p. 148.
38. Thaler, "Toward a Positive Theory . . . ," p. 11. This is not fully clear. Thaler doesn't want to say that $I_{b'}$ may not be flatter than I_b, that how much of *x* is *had* may never "affect decisions."
39. Thaler, "The Psychology of Choice . . . ," p. 142.
40. The Newcomb story first appeared in Robert Nozick, "Newcomb's Problem and Two Principles of Choice," in Nicholas Rescher et al. (eds.), *Essays in Honor of Carl G. Hempel*, Dordrecht: Reidel, 1969. In the initial story, E is one-boxing and F is two-boxing.
41. This analysis applies to just the usual sort of Newcomb issues, in which the outcomes are factorable into endogenous and exogenous gains and losses. (These need not be monetary; see my *Understanding Action*, pp. 142–3.) A problem in which they can't be so factored is noted in John Broome, "An Economic Newcomb Problem," *Analysis* 49 (1989).
42. Figure 3.3 shows that too, as indeed Figure 3.6 also shows a diminishing sensitivity to gains and losses *of x*.
43. It may be suggested that primary assets are those that are valued "for their own sake." But this would be too strong and could not help us much anyway.

ESSAY 4

1. I argue this in my *Making Choices,* Cambridge: Cambridge University Press, 1997. Also in my *Understanding Action,* Cambridge: Cambridge University Press, 1991, and throughout in this book.
2. Where the situation is action *a*, *p* might be that *a is of sort b*.
3. The belief need not *precede* the seeing. We may see some situation as *p* as soon as we come to believe *p*.
4. I have more to say on this matter in Essay 6.
5. Often a persuasion is taken to be our getting some other to *do* what we want. I will say we persuade him to *do a* where we persuade him to *see a* in a way that then gives him a reason to do it. (Likewise for our *convincing* him or *inducing* him to do it.)
6. Herman Melville, *The Shorter Novels of Herman Melville,* New York: Liveright, 1942, pp. 303–4.
7. Here I apply an analysis of choices as comings-to-want; see my *Making Choices,* pp. 11–12.
8. Relating this to my concept of reasons: *d* is their desire to take an action of sort *b*, *d′* is their desire to take an action of sort *b′*.
9. In Essay 6, the wiring-up of *d* is discussed in terms of the salience of propositions reporting the satisfaction of *d*.
10. Here *p* reports the satisfaction of *d* (i.e., it is *d is satisfied*) and *p′* reports the satisfaction of *d′*.
11. You believe *p* and *q* coreportive where 1: you believe $p \equiv q$, 2: $p \equiv q$ follows from some propositions you believe about self-identities (*inter alia*), and 3: these latter propositions follow from neither *p* nor *q*. For more on this concept, see *Understanding Action,* pp. 74–7.
12. "Values" is an umbrella-term here, a way of speaking of desires and preferences and utilities collectively. I take no stand on what (if anything) all these have in common.
13. In *Understanding Action* and in *Making Choices;* also in my "Attending to Understandings," *Journal of Philosophy* 89 (1992).
14. Daniel Kahneman and Amos Tversky, "Choices, Values and Frames," *American Psychologist* 39 (1984), p. 344.
15. Isaac Levi, "A Note on Newcombmania," *Journal of Philosophy* 79 (1982), p. 342.
16. As in ". . . I shall assume that goods [i.e., values] are strongly extensional" (Jonathan Baron, *Morality and Rational Choice,* Dordrecht: Kluwer, 1993, p. 32).

17. Nelson Goodman, *Fact, Fiction, and Forecast*, 4th ed., Cambridge, MA: Harvard University Press, 1983, p. 64. Goodman has "rules" and "inferences" in place of my "principles" and "judgments."
18. I say more about equilibria in Essay 6.
19. Note that not all propositions about some *s* are coreportive of it.
20. It is proposed in Brian Skyrms's review of my *Making Choices* in *TLS (Times Literary Supplement)*, Feb. 6, 1998, and also in William J. Talbott's review of that book in *Mind* 110 (2001).
21. Donald Davidson, "How Is Weakness of the Will Possible?," in his *Essays on Actions and Events*, Oxford: Oxford University Press, 1980.
22. For more on selectivity, see the Essay 3 discussion of status-quo versus total-assets basing; also Essays 1 and 7.
23. In his *Fact, Fiction, and Forecast*, Chapter 3. See also Essay 2 in this book.
24. The rest is his analysis of why we now see things as we do.
25. It is adapted from Davidson, *op. cit.*, p. 40 (his analysis of "all things considered").
26. This paragraph and the next are taken from my *Understanding Action*, pp. 153–4.
27. Aristotle, *Nichomachean Ethics*, 1143[a]. I discuss Aristotle's theory of reasoning in *Understanding Action*, pp. 55–60.
28. Immanuel Kant, *Critique of Pure Reason*, A133, B172. For more on Kant on seeings, see *Understanding Action*, pp. 65–70.
29. This recalls Quine's take on Goodman; see W. V. Quine, "Natural Kinds," in his *Ontological Relativity and Other Essays*, New York: Columbia University Press, 1969.
30. The first if-then is logic, the second is integrity: unless you have a reason for not doing what you want to do, do it!
31. Jane Austen, *Persuasion*, Harmondsworth: Penguin, 1965, pp. 42, 55–6.
32. Does this give us a handle on our approval of *blue*-wise seeings and not *bleen*-wise seeings? Perhaps, if we want to be the sort of person whose seeings resemble those that have figured in successful predictions in the past. (Goodman explores this idea.)
33. W. V. Quine, "Two Dogmas of Empiricism," in his *From a Logical Point of View*, 2nd ed., Cambridge, MA: Harvard University Press, 1980, pp. 42–3.
34. For a broad-scope equilibrium test of this sort, see Essay 6.
35. Austin, *Persuasion*, p. 248.

36. The corresponding question for Quine is that of what an *experience* is.
37. For these matters, see Harry G. Frankfurt, "The Importance of What We Care About," in his *The Importance of What We Care About*, Cambridge: Cambridge University Press, 1988, and his "On the Usefulness of Final Ends" and "On Caring," in his *Necessity, Volition, and Love*, Cambridge: Cambridge University Press, 1999.

ESSAY 5

1. Imagine a second subscript to the "*B*"s identifying the believer – in this case, the student.
2. Strictly, it moves to its second stage; the proof began with our supposing (1). The depth of their indentation mark the levels of our suppositions.
3. We need this in moving from (9) and (10) to (11) and also in moving from (15) to (16).
4. As a general principle, belief retention is too strong. It rules out all changing of minds on the basis of a rethinking of the evidence – on the basis of nothing "new." Still, in our cases, that won't make for trouble.
5. This simpler case is in W. V. Quine, "On a So-Called Paradox," *Mind* 62 (1953). Even simpler is G. E. Moore's case of the person who says it is raining but that he doesn't (now!) believe it – or is told this about himself by someone else (the teacher).
6. In the second scenario, we are assuming discipline in the move from (22) to (23).
7. Jaakko Hintikka, *Knowledge and Belief*, Ithaca: Cornell University Press, 1962.
8. This is different from the basic exclusion of both believing and not-believing *p*.
9. Since *p* and *q* are *propositions*, *doing p* and *taking action p* must be understood as *making p true*.
10. For more on optionality, see my *Making Choices*, Cambridge: Cambridge University Press, 1997, pp. 8–11.
11. It must have been an option *as I saw it*; see my *Making Choices*, pp. 11–21. No need here to press this refinement, but it is often useful.
12. Deductive thoroughness is implicit in the move from (30) and (32) to (33). Retentiveness is implicit in the move from (31) to (32).

13. This point was made in Karl R. Popper, "Indeterminism in Quantum Physics and in Classical Physics," *British Journal for the Philosophy of Science* 1 (1950).
14. The logic of forgetting is discussed in Hans K. Hvide, "Bounds to Memory Loss," *Theory and Decision* 46 (1999).
15. If she told him and believed he believed her (and believed him disciplined), it would be out of bounds for her too: she would have to doubt what she told him. See the "further consequence" near the end of Section 1.
16. This is a special case, since Jack need not be disciplined here. The moves from (38) reflect *our* going by logic, not Jack's.
17. Some improper beliefs are only indirectly self-referential. Think of the anti-mentalist theorist who believes that there are no beliefs.
18. For that logic, see Essay 6. Strictly, the logic of the present essay is that logic plus belief retention.
19. I discuss the Prisoners' Dilemma in Essay 2.
20. In Essay 2, I reject that analysis.
21. In terms of our own beliefs, if we believe (accept) CB, the backward induction requires us to believe that Jack believes $C_{99}d$. $C_{99}d$ is incredible for Jack, so (if we believe him to be disciplined) we ourselves must believe it is false – recall the "further consequence" in Section 1. But CB and the backward induction require us to believe it true.
22. We cannot give up the assumption of the parties being disciplined. The backward induction depends on that; it depends on thoroughness.
23. The observer can predict both joint-defection and joint-*choosing-to*-defect.
24. It may be that even RB is too strong; this is implicit in the critique of CB in Philip Pettit and Robert Sugden, "The Backward Induction Paradox," *Journal of Philosophy* 86 (1989), and in Cristina Bicchieri, *Rationality and Coordination*, Cambridge: Cambridge University Press, 1993. If RB is too strong, the backward induction still can't be worked, but not now because the parties have to hold improper beliefs.
25. They are speaking not of common belief but of common *knowledge*; see their "Common Knowledge and Game Theory," in Binmore's *Essays on the Foundations of Game Theory*, Oxford: Blackwell, 1990, p. 106. But common knowledge implies common belief.

26. John Rawls, *A Theory of Justice*, Cambridge, MA: Harvard University Press, 1971, p. 56. Again, though Rawls speaks of common knowledge, that implies common belief.
27. *Op. cit.*, p. 142.
28. Better, p and q... are options for these people collectively only. An individual chooser's options p', q'... are *to vote for p, to vote for q*....
29. This isn't all there is to the matter. See my *Making Choices*, pp. 71–2.
30. The argument appeals to a wanting-extension of our concept of discipline. Thoroughness and consistency carry over smoothly, but retention now needs some refining. (You go to bed, wanting to sleep; when you wake up, you no longer do, though you have no new "pertinent information." Are you being undisciplined?)
31. Immanuel Kant, *Fundamental Principles of the Metaphysic of Morals*, New York: Liberal Arts Press, 1949, p. 38.
32. In Essay 4, I argue that to act on desire d is to take some action that we believe satisfies d where we *see* that action as one that satisfies d.
33. This refers only to commonality of degree 1, not to any CB-sort iterations.
34. Reciprocity of degree 1.
35. See note 30.
36. This may well be too strong; I suggest it with reservations.

ESSAY 6

1. Not your usual logic if you object to quantifying into belief contexts. If you do, skip this proof; the others involve no quantification.
2. It derives from G. E. Moore.
3. Where, as here, I speak of logical principles, I use "x" and "y"... in place of "p" and "q"....
4. The first line of the proof becomes $\sim p \cdot B{\sim}{\sim}p$, a new second line is $\sim p \cdot Bp$ (by thoroughness), and the rest (from 13 on) has $\sim p$ in place of p and p in place of $\sim p$.
5. If Jack is disciplined, $\sim$ (24) must be false, for then $\sim$ (24) implies $Bq \cdot {\sim}Bq$. So, if he is disciplined, $\sim(24) \cdot B{\sim}(24)$ must be false, which means that $B{\sim}(24) \supset (24)$.
6. Applied to *necessity*, they are often labeled *5* (or *E*), *T*, *K*, and *PL*. See Brian F. Chellas, *Modal Logic*, Cambridge: Cambridge University

Press, 1980, p. 14, and G. E. Hughes and M. J. Cresswell, *A Companion to Modal Logic*, London: Methuen, 1984, pp. 4–11.

7. The discipline that figures in a propriety concept is always of a narrowly local sort. In the concept of proper *belief*, it is belief-thoroughness and belief-consistency; in that of proper *wanting*, it is desire-thoroughness and desire-consistency, etc.
8. Since only propositions serve here as tokens, the probability settings .6 and .5 are distinct propositional attitudes, not the same attitude differently tokened (tokened, in part, by decimals).
9. I argue that in most of the essays in this book.
10. In particular, in Essay 4.
11. For the argument *re* utility maximization, see my *Making Choices*, Cambridge: Cambridge University Press, 1997, p. 131. For that *re* the probability and preference principles, see my "Dutch Bookies and Money Pumps," *Journal of Philosophy* 83 (1986). For that *re* induction, see Jerrold J. Katz, *The Problem of Induction and its Solution*, Chicago: University of Chicago Press, 1962.
12. Donald Davidson takes certain principles to present what "may be viewed as constitutive of the range of applications of such concepts as those of belief, desire . . . "; this in his "Psychology as Philosophy," in his *Essays on Actions and Events*, Oxford: Oxford University Press, 1980, p. 237.
13. This is Jerry A. Fodor's position in a long sequence of books from *The Language of Thought*, Cambridge, MA: Harvard University Press, 1975, to *The Mind Doesn't Work That Way*, Cambridge, MA: MIT Press, 2000.
14. In Goodman's *Fact, Fiction, and Forecast*, 4th ed., Cambridge, MA: Harvard University Press, 1983, p. 64. (The term "reflective equilibrium" is John Rawls's.)
15. More narrowly, the set is accepted if, given our beliefs *tokened by propositions about certain tokened attitudes*, ... The judgment above depends on my believing that *Jack believes p*. Other judgments may depend on my believing that *I believe p* or on my believing that *I want p*, etc.
16. Thus thoroughness moves us from (8) to (9), but only given the logic that says that $p \cdot {\sim}Bp$ implies p.
17. An ancestor of this point appears in C. L. Dodgson (Lewis Carroll), "What the Tortoise Said to Achilles," *Mind* 4 (1895).
18. What is this directive "must" (and the "ought" above)? Is it the same as that of ethics? And what does "faulting" mean here? These issues I am setting aside.

19. See my *Understanding Action*, Cambridge: Cambridge University Press, 1991, pp. 77–8.
20. Replacing *B*-thoroughness with *B,E*-thoroughness calls for either some weakening of the proofs that take off from (7) and (12) or for adopting certain *E*-principles (such that if you entertain $x \cdot y$, you must entertain x, and if you entertain $\sim x$, you must entertain x, and if you entertain $x \supset y$, you must entertain y).
21. For this concept, see my *Making Choices*, pp. 71–3.
22. Without the "neither-*x*-nor..." clause, if you believed p (or $p \cdot p'$) and wanted any q, you would have to want p (or p'). The corresponding proviso in my *Understanding Action* (p. 50) was too strong; this was noted by Christian Piller in his review of that book in *Erkenntnis* 41 (1994).
23. The labeling of a plural-attitude principle mentions the attitude it directs us to first. *D,B*-thoroughness calls for the *wanting* of *z*, so it is *D,B*- . . . , not *B,D*-thoroughness.
24. Rejecting these extensionality principles doesn't require rejecting those whose antecedents are "if *x* and *y* are *logically equivalent*. . . . "
25. This appears in Essay 1. I comment on it also in my *Understanding Action*, pp. 1ff passim.
26. That is, *In making-true x, I would make-true y.*
27. The *S*-clause replaces the *E*-clause here. If you make salient *In z'ing, I would y*, you must be entertaining *z*.
28. I take this case from Amartya Sen's "Rationality and Uncertainty," *Theory and Decision* 18 (1985). The hiring story of Essay 1 could have been used here too.
29. Where you help Jill (where you don't toss that coin), there are of course no heads or tails. So we have to read c_1 and c_2 as "The coin would fall heads / fall tails *if you tossed it*."
30. Why not require only that y_1 and y_2 . . . and y_n be salient? Because no proposition can be salient unless it is believed, and you don't (yet) believe any of these. (You won't until you choose what to do and you learn which *c*-state holds.) But perhaps we might require that you think y_1 and y_2 . . . *would* be salient *if* you believed these propositions.
31. U^+-expectedness refers to the probabilities of the contingencies $c_1, c_2, \ldots c_n$, but since probabilities are propositional attitudes, this comes down to the probabilities of propositions reporting those contingencies. Still, we needn't add a clause requiring that these propositions be salient too, for that would be vacuous if (as is

likely) we accept the extensionality *of probabilities*, the principle that whoever thinks x and y coreportive must set the same *probability* on them.

32. U^+-expectedness and D^+-expectedness may be thought too weak, for they only apply where the utilities and probabilities are point-precise. Where these are vague (are *not* point-precise), the principles need to be generalized, perhaps along the lines of my *Making Choices*, pp. 44–8. See also Essay 2, where I speak of vagueness as *uncertainty*.
33. For the commensurability issue, see Ruth Chang (ed.), *Incommensurability, Incomparability, and Practical Reason*, Cambridge, MA: Harvard University Press, 1997.
34. In other essays in this book, univocity is taken to be definitive of salience.

ESSAY 7

1. Leo Tolstoy, *Anna Karenina*, New York: Grosset and Dunlap, n.d., pp. 471–2.
2. Both quotes are from *Anna Karenina*, p. 476.
3. *Ecclesiastes* 2:14–17.
4. Probabilities may enter here for him, but we needn't consider that now.
5. A person's utility scale is the range of all the utilities he sets, not just of those he sets on what he might now *do*.
6. Speaking of people's utilities lets me put this idea concisely, but we needn't think that a person always has a utility scale and utility distribution. Everything here could be put (less clearly) in non-utility terms.
7. Let o be the outcome-conjunction of Levin's doing x, and o' that of his *not* doing x. Let d be that Levin will die, a part of both o and o'. For Levin, whatever the action x, $u(o) \simeq u(d)$ and also $u(o') \simeq u(d)$, and thus $u(o) \simeq u(o')$. Thus also $u(x) \simeq u(\sim x)$.
8. Quoted by Rosemary Edmonds in her introduction to her translation of *Anna Karenin* [*sic*], Harmondsworth: Penguin, 1954.
9. They then also count as sequels: what *would be true* if we did x (the atemporal sequel) takes in all that has happened.

10. The *lowness* too of these utilities is relative to his utility scale.
11. *Ecclesiastes* 9:11.
12. *Op. cit.*, 1:9.
13. Some writers lay out the "deeper" problem in wholly secular terms; for the loss of God they put the collapse of moral realism. For instance, see Albert Camus, *The Myth of Sisyphus*, New York: Vintage, 1959.
14. F. P. Ramsey, "Epilogue," in his *Philosophical Papers* (D. H. Mellor, ed.), Cambridge: Cambridge University Press, 1990, p. 249.
15. J. S. Bach, Cantata No. 4: "Christ Lay in the Bonds of Death," verses 3 and 4.
16. Let o be the outcome-conjunction of the Christian's doing x, and o' that of his *not* doing x. Let e be that eternal life awaits him. The Christian takes both o and o' to include e, and so, for him, whatever x is, $u(o) \simeq u(e)$ and $u(o') \simeq u(e)$. Thus $u(o) \simeq u(o')$ and also $u(x) \simeq u(\sim x)$, but the Christian has bliss.
17. For a full discussion, see Peter D. Kramer, *Listening to Prozac*, Harmondsworth: Penguin, 1997.
18. Tolstoy must leave some slack on the margin, else why would he care what Levin thinks?
19. The best report of Tolstoy's views on these matters is Isaiah Berlin's "The Hedgehog and the Fox" in Berlin's *Russian Thinkers*, Harmondsworth: Penguin, 1994.
20. *Anna Karenina*, pp. 1053–5.
21. *Op. cit.*, p. 1055.
22. *Op. cit.*, p. 1063.
23. *Op. cit.*, p. 1060.
24. Tolstoy himself went into despair *after* writing *Anna Karenina*. He reports that part of his life in *A Confession*, Harmondsworth: Penguin, 1987.
25. This idea is developed in my *Making Choices*, Cambridge: Cambridge University Press, 1997, and in my *Understanding Action*, Cambridge: Cambridge University Press, 1991. See also Essay 6 (on U^+-expectedness).
26. *Anna Karenina*, p. 1062.
27. Epictetus, *Discourses*, in Whitney J. Oates (ed.), *The Stoic and Epicurean Philosophers*, New York: Random House, 1940, pp. 225, 447–8.
28. *Ecclesiastes*, 9:7–10.

29. The Preacher's message is discussed in Elias Bickerman, *Four Strange Books of the Bible*, New York: Schocken, 1967, pp. 139–68.
30. "What is your aim in philosophy? – To show the fly out of the fly-bottle." Ludwig Wittgenstein, *Philosophical Investigations*, Oxford: Blackwell, 1958, #309.
31. I borrow this case from my *Understanding Action*, p. 157ff.
32. Claude Lanzmann, *Shoah*, New York: Pantheon, 1985, p. 183.

INDEX